CONTENTS

COLOR PLATES

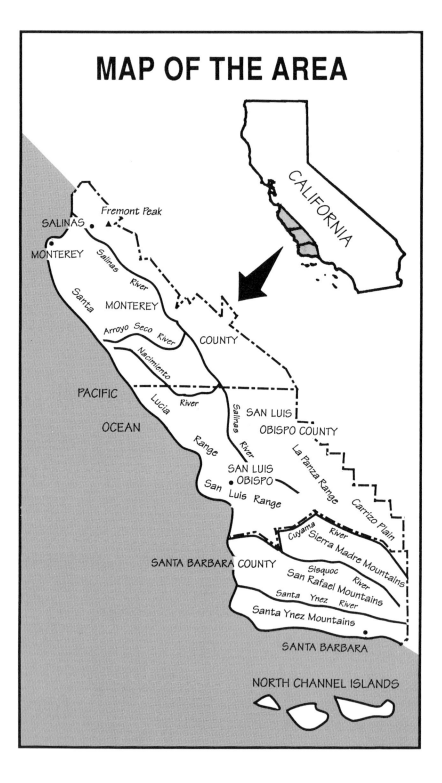

MAP OF THE AREA

CALIFORNIA

Fremont Peak

SALINAS

MONTEREY

Salinas River

Santa

MONTEREY

Arroyo Seco River

COUNTY

Nacimiento River

PACIFIC

Lucia

Salinas River

SAN LUIS

OCEAN

Range

OBISPO COUNTY

La Panza Range

SAN LUIS
OBISPO

San Luis Range

Carrizo Plain

Cuyama River

Sierra Madre Mountains

SANTA BARBARA COUNTY

Sisquoc River

San Rafael Mountains

Santa Ynez River

Santa Ynez Mountains

SANTA BARBARA

NORTH CHANNEL ISLANDS

PARTS OF A FLOWER

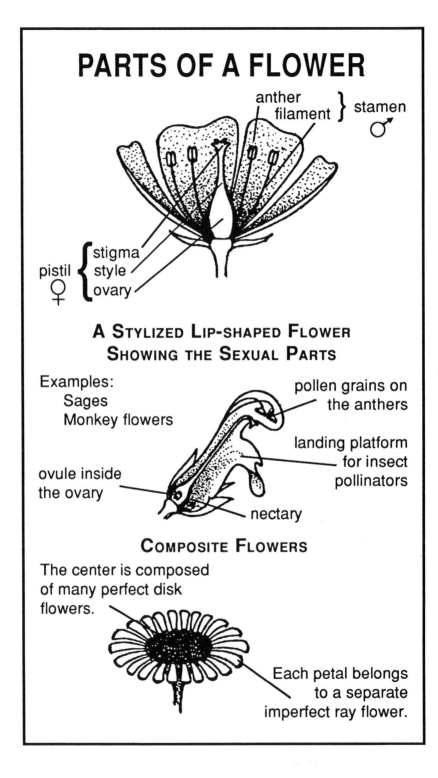

anther
filament } stamen ♂

pistil ♀ { stigma
style
ovary

**A STYLIZED LIP-SHAPED FLOWER
SHOWING THE SEXUAL PARTS**

Examples:
    Sages
    Monkey flowers

pollen grains on
    the anthers

landing platform
    for insect
    pollinators

ovule inside
the ovary

nectary

COMPOSITE FLOWERS

The center is composed
of many perfect disk
flowers.

Each petal belongs
    to a separate
    imperfect ray flower.

ACKNOWLEDGMENTS

Two docents at the Morro Bay Natural History Museum, **Gloria Walter** and **Eileen Zolkoski**, should get credit for inspiring this book. They saw its need to fill a large gap in the material available for this area. They encouraged me to write it and Eileen's husband **Ed Zolkoski** to publish it. He has also edited it and **Sharon Lewis Dickerson** pushed what I wrote (and Ed Z. agreed to!) through her computer again, again and yet again. I am truly grateful for their skills.

Shirley Sparling and **Malcolm McLeod**, professors at Cal Poly and associates in the activities of the California Native Plant Society as well as companions in the flower fields, edited the manuscript and offered many helpful changes which have improved the book. I especially appreciated this level of editing.

Most of the colored pictures are from the author's collection. In addition, the following friends and trail companions have given permission to use their photos:

C. J. and Virgene Engberg: Chocolate Lily (C-8)

David Gibbs: Sand Plant (C-7)

Susan Grimaud: Buckeye (C-14)

Harvey Hess: Santa Lucia Fir (C-9)

Dorothy Irvin: Madrone (C-7, left)

Beverly Sessa: Gray Pine (close-up, C-10); Hummingbird Sage (habit view, C-10); Sticky Phacelia (C-12); Indian Paintbrush (C-19)

Gloria and Ed Walter: Ceanothus (Front flap, bottom); Two views of Giant Coreopsis (C-2); Lupine (C-2); Twinberry (C-7); Hummingbird Sage (close-up, C-10)

The black-and-white drawings also came from a variety of sources:

Glenn Drewes, artist and biologist, prepared the diagram, "Parts of a Flower," page VII.

The redwood environment diagram on page 122 was drawn by **Gerhard Bakker** for *An Island Called California* by Elna S. Bakker.

Twenty-five drawings were provided by Cambria artist and botanist **Linda Warren Seek**. The rest of the drawings were reproduced with the kind permission of the **University of California Press** and the **Jepson Herbarium**, both at Berkeley, and **Stanford University Press**. A detailed list may be found on page 159.

PREFACE

My intent in writing this book is to share with flower-lovers the gleanings of a lifetime of discovery, observation and inquiry about flowering plants, their names and how they manage to live where we find them. Having been a general science teacher, mountain trail naturalist and natural history docent, I've written as I speak in the out-of-doors, using non-technical language as much as possible. There is a basic glossary in the back. We chose to include mainly the showy, readily found wildflowers of Monterey, San Luis Obispo and Santa Barbara Counties, a relatively unspoiled area of pastoral valleys, small rugged mountain ranges and spectacular coastline, midway between the megalopoli of San Francisco and Los Angeles. I have lived here fourteen years and love hiking and reveling in our parks, forests and wilderness reserves.

The wildflowers are grouped in eleven chapters according to natural divisions or "lumped" plant communities, beginning at the seashore and moving inland. While we have listed each plant in only one community, quite a few are also found in others, as for example California poppies. There is a complete index behind the glossary which includes the common (often more than one) and genus names of all the wildflowers discussed and their page numbers.

I wish to thank all the nameless park ranger-naturalists, teachers, seminar leaders and fellow nature lovers who have shared their knowledge and enthusiasm with me by the sea, in the fields and mountains and beside streams of our wonderful wild California.

Writing this book has been fun and also hard work and I grew a little in the process. I don't suppose many of us expect to grow much after age seventy, so I'm glad I was asked to write it and was permitted to organize it according to my perception of the grand natural world that still remains around us in this time and place. I truly hope readers will join me and other environmentalists in respecting and protecting this dynamic living world that supports all life on our planet.

—*Mary Coffeen*

INTRODUCTION

There ought to be someone like Mary Coffeen in every nature center, on every interpretive trail and in every state and national parkland in California. Since this is unlikely, let this delightful introduction to wildflowers of California's central coast be your companion. Exploring natural landscapes as diverse as kelp beds and oak woodlands, Mary gently leads you towards understanding the whys and hows of plant adaptation—the ability of plants to adjust to the many conditions of soil, climate and interaction with other living things imposed by a particular environment.

Why is sand verbena sticky? Would you believe that its glandular hairs excrete a substance to which sand grains adhere, forming a tough coating that shields the vulnerable tissue inside? How about the field of California poppies that was so showy yesterday and today is nothing but a pale gleam on an overcast day? Mary explains that this is an example of how flowers respond to changes in sunlight. The poppies, reacting to a possible rainshower, fold their bright petals over the reproductive parts in the center of the flower, protecting them from weather damage.

Though treating wildflowers, the star performers of wildland dramas, with loving care, Mary does not neglect insects and other often-unappreciated supporting members of the cast. She is a conscientious bee-watcher, enjoying their acrobatics as they maneuver their way out of woolly blue-curls or crowd over wild buckwheat in a "bee picnic."

The book has many helpful hints about growing native plants in your garden, a chancy business to many of us. This book is by no means a guide to their propagation, but it has numerous practical suggestions about successfully cultivating native species.

A bit of advice. Invest in a hand lens so that you can see for yourself the entrancing details Mary describes so invitingly. Look for that groove in the lupine's banner whose color guides bees to nectarous pay-dirt. Identify certain California lilacs by checking for hairs on the leaves.

There is a wonderful world out there waiting for you. Accept Mary's invitation and see it through her eyes.

—*Elna S. Bakker*
noted ecologist and author of
An Island Called California

GOLDFIELDS–PAGE 100

TIDY TIPS–PAGE 79

DEERWEED–PAGE 24

SAND VERBENA–PAGE 4

FREMONTIA–PAGE 48

SEA THRIFT—PAGE 17

GIANT COREOPSIS—PAGE 11

LUPINE—PAGE 5

GIANT COREOPSIS—PAGE 11

Blue-Eyed Grass and

Blazing Star—Page 74

Buttercup—Pages 22, 130

Beach Primrose—Page 8

Poison Oak in Spring—Page 31

Poison Oak in Autumn—Page 31

Persian Carpet at Shell Creek—Page 67

Wild Iris—Page 14

WILD SWEETPEA–PAGE 45

BIRD'S EYE GILIA–PAGE 81

THISTLE SAGE–PAGE 93

WOOLLY STAR–PAGE 40

Coast Live Oak–Page 68

Bush Poppy–Page 51

MADRONE FLOWERS—PAGE 123

MADRONE TREE—PAGE 123

MADRONE BERRIES—PAGE 123

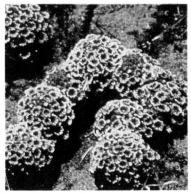

SAND PLANT—PAGE 9

TWINBERRY—PAGE 111

CHOCOLATE LILY—PAGE 33

FOOTSTEPS OF SPRING—PAGE 18

BIG LEAF MAPLE–PAGE 109

SANTA LUCIA FIR–PAGE 127

FAIRY LANTERN–PAGE 116

COTTONWOOD–PAGE 104

HUMMINGBIRD SAGE—PAGE 28

HUMMINGBIRD SAGE—PAGE 28

GRAY PINE—PAGE 89

GRAY PINE—PAGE 89

WOOLLY BLUE CURLS—PAGE 59

WOOLLY BLUE CURLS—PAGE 59

Tanbark Oak–Page 126

Clematis–Page 60

CALIFORNIA POPPY–PAGE 13

STICKY PHACELIA–PAGE 38

OBISPO MARIPOSA–PAGE 84

BUSH MONKEY FLOWER–PAGE 38

WET BUMBLEBEE

POLLINATOR ON FLOWER

BEE'S EYE VIEW OF POPPY—PAGE 13

WALLFLOWER—PAGE 94

MARIPOSA LILY—PAGE 83

BUCKEYE—PAGE 91

JOHNNY-JUMP-UP—PAGE 94

SEEP MONKEY FLOWER—PAGE 114

CALIFORNIA HONEYSUCKLE–PAGE 129

RED MAIDS–PAGE 141   PINK-FLOWERING CURRANT–PAGE 56

VERNAL POOL–PAGE 137

Live-Forever--Page 18

Chaparral Pea--Page 46

Chia—Page 27

Wild Cucumber—Page 33

California Fuchsia—Page 34

Purple Nightshade—Page 119

Matilija Poppy—Page 61

STAR LILY–PAGE 24

SEA ROCKET–PAGE 3

STAR LILY–PAGE 24

INDIAN WARRIOR–PAGE 58

Toyon—Page 55

Scarlet Bugler—Page 85

Indian Paintbrush—Page 101

Climbing Penstemon—Page 52

Crimson Columbine—Page 116

YERBA SANTA—PAGE 29

WINE CUPS—PAGE 83

PRICKLY PHLOX—PAGE 61

POLLINATOR AT WORK

BABY BLUE EYES—PAGE 80

SAND VERBENA—PAGE 4

CHECKER BLOOM—PAGE 19

ELEGANT CLARKIA—PAGE 82

SHOOTING STAR—PAGE 100

BEACH MORNING GLORY—PAGE 7

SAND VERBENA AND BUSH LUPINE—PAGES 4, 5

WILD ROSE—PAGE 30

1. SUBMARINE FOREST

GIANT KELP—*Macrocystis pyrifera*

Seaweeds are found in abundance in the near-shore ocean the whole length of our three counties of the central coast. Many of us use the words kelp and algae perhaps too freely. In the interest of accuracy, note that most seaweeds and all kelp are algae. We often see their discards—massive tangles of brown rubbery stipes, blades and holdfasts—as we walk the beaches, especially after a storm at sea. They are vitally important in complex food webs of natural life in the sea and on the beaches. They are here because of off-shore winds and currents that carry surface water away from the shore causing cold water from below to rise. These upwelling waters are rich in mineral nutrients that these plants need to live.

We shall mention only the giant kelp, *Macrocystis pyrifera*, as an example of seaweeds. It is the large brown algae group of seaweeds. It is the fastest growing (14 inches or more a day) of the many submarine forest plants. Giant kelp's **holdfast** is not a true root in that it does not supply food to the plant, but effectively anchors this huge plant tightly to the rocky seafloor; its stubby intertwined branches provide food and shelter for many creatures in its niche. **Stipes** are similar to land plants' stems, but instead of being stiff, they are tough and elastic so they can sway back and forth in the surging ocean. They also play a nutritional transportation role between the holdfast below and the blades above.

Some stipes develop hollow structures called **floats**. They fill with air which provides buoyancy. Giant kelp has a float at the base of most blades lifting them up toward the sunlit waters at the surface. **Blades** of giant kelp are the main food factories for this huge marine plant. Blade cells absorb water, carbon dioxide and other chemicals from the seawater and, using energy from the sun, they convert these chemicals into oxygen and food compounds—sugar, amino acids and other building blocks of the plant. These foods nourish all parts of the kelp from the growing tips up in the canopy to holdfasts below and the many developing blades in between. Extra food, besides that required for the plant's maintenance, is stored in the cells, making all parts of the plant nutritious meals for countless invertebrates and fish. "Photosynthesis, this art of using sunlight to make food," nourishes the plants that support all the rest of life in our world including us. Also some small blades down by the holdfast produce spores which ensure future generations of giant kelp.

We hope this brief look at the life of giant kelp will tempt you to inquire further into the wonderful marine world by personal observation, reading and visits to the splendid Monterey Bay Aquarium. There you can stand dry while watching giant kelp sway with its many associates in the surging seawater in the kelp forest exhibit—a rich and unparalleled opportunity.

2. BEACH DUNES

SEA ROCKET—*Cakile maritima*

Pretend for a moment that you've just swum ashore from a shipwreck onto a natural beach. The first living thing you find might well be this little mustard plant. With succulent green stems and leaves and pert lavender-pink four-petaled flowers, it sprawls here and there just above the high tide line. It's fun to find the inch high seedlings on the strand and up into the foredunes after the winter rains have begun, often January in our area. They seem to be all stems and two seed leaves. But walk around until you find a more mature plant that has summered over with stored moisture and fog drip.

Below the new flowers on the stem you'll find the rockets. These, of course, are the part of the flowers that become the seed pods. Cut one open lengthwise and find one to several large (for the mustard family) seeds. Encased in their pods, these seeds can survive floating in sea water up to eleven days and wash up on another shore. Once there, winter rains leach the fruits of salt and they germinate and grow where time and conditions are right.

The seed pods may resemble some rockets, but they are not shot into the sea by the plant. The mature pods are dry, light in weight and break off the stem at the line you can easily see. The seeds above the line are the potential travelers, those below the line probably will grow close by the original plant. They tumble around on the sand and some make it into the waves. Nature's dispersal methods may seem rather casual to us, but they work. The genus name of sea rocket is Arabic—a distant shore indeed.

Field research at Bodega Head Marine Lab has documented sea rocket's rapid dispersal along California shores after arriving in 1935. During the next 40-odd years they migrated north and south along the Pacific Coast at an average rate of 33 miles per year. Around 1973 the range had extended from the Queen Charlotte Islands, British Columbia, to Cedros Island off Baja California, a distance of nearly 2000 miles! So watch for this hardy, well-traveled plant on the beaches through the seasons and come to better understand its adaptations by reading more about sea rockets in *Coastal Ecology* included in our Further Reading List.

SAND VERBENA—*Abronia maritima,* *A. latifolia* and *A. umbellata*

A. maritima   A. umbellata

These handsome perennials grow along our shores usually in these colors: rose-violet—*A. maritima,* yellow—*A. latifolia* and a variable purple through rose to white one—*A. umbellata.* The first two pioneer on the flat beaches, on the first sand hillocks (helping them to build) and further back in the older high dunes. The third is less succulent than the first two and may also be found behind the dunes in the coastal scrub, as at Shark Inlet on the southern extremity of Morro Bay. The bright flowers appear on the sprangly stems which may wander ten feet over the sand. All three have made some interesting adaptations to the wind-blown sand where they live. They have long fleshy roots (you may have found these exposed where a hillock has shifted) and a prostrate growth habit which keeps them below the fiercest wind. The yellow and rose-violet verbenas that live closest to the sea also have fleshy leaves and stems which have sticky glandular hairs. These glands exude a substance to which the grains of sand adhere, forming an armor-like coating which shields the succulent vegetative cells inside.

The attached sand grains may double the weight of the plant, which also helps to hold it down in a blow. You may discover a less obvious adaptation if you come upon verbena growing on a creek-mouth beach with cobblestones on and in the sand. I did, soon after a storm at high tide which had rearranged much of the surface. There were sand verbenas standing up six or eight inches high on thick tan stalks. I could hardly believe they were verbenas, but more knowledgeable companions encouraged me to look carefully at the leaves and seed pods (which resemble small hairy grenades) and I was, of course, convinced. These long, heavy roots serve the plant well for storing its products of photosynthesis and providing firm anchorage even among rocks in a habitat prone to change.

Vernon L. Human, who writes occasionally for the "People for the Nipomo Dunes" newsletter, tells a fascinating story of how in the spring of 1989 he found out who pollinates sand verbenas in his area. He discovered that the creature's sucking equipment and the size and shape of the floral tube were a "perfect fit" for each other. I put this in to pique your curiosity to get out there on a warm quiet spring day and find out for yourself, as I intend to do!

LUPINE—*Lupinus* spp.

Blue, purple, white and yellow. Widely occurring in several habitats, they make blue "lakes" in the oak woodlands, join with other spring annuals to make "Persian carpets" in open meadows and make soaring swatches of blue on the spring-green ridges of the coast ranges. Yellow lupine has been used along the coast to bind blowing sand along highways. The yellow lupine is probably an introduced species, believed first planted by a lighthouse keeper's wife near Eureka, California, in 1917.

Lupines have a lot going for them besides beauty and sometimes fragrance. At the shore where rainwater drains rapidly away through the sand, their deep roots follow it down to freshwater pools that form at groundwater level where it tends not to mix with the denser saltwater. Like many members of the Pea Family, lupines store nitrogen in nodules on their roots, enriching their hillocks and thus making it possible for additional plants to grow and add to the stabilizing of the dunes.

It's fascinating to look closely at a single lupine flower. The banner (upper petal) has a groove often with a contrasting color to guide a nectar-seeking bee. As it probes to the base, the bee's weight on the lower petals causes the anthers in the keel to spread their pollen on the insect's hairy body. Some lupines signal their pollinators not to come in as their nectar supply wanes by changing the color of that banner area from white to rose-blue.

Perennials such as silver lupine—*L. chamissonis*—and bush lupine—*L. arboreus*—may be found in the coastal scrub usually farther back from the sea than most annuals. With their woody bases, extensive network of roots and robust foliage, they have a longer and later blooming period than the annual species which go through the whole life cycle, from seed to seed, every year.

BEACH STRAWBERRY—*Fragaria chiloensis*

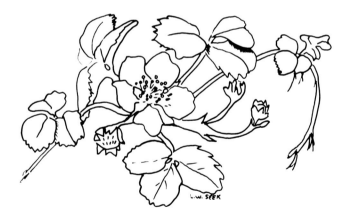

These lovely, fragrant, white-petaled flowers are real harbingers of spring in the dunes. (A little later, *F. californica* blooms in the woods of the coastal ranges in our counties.)

Beach strawberry, with its stout rootstocks, bright red runners that root at the nodes, and three leaflets, begins to stabilize moving sand in the early stages of dune succession. Also with their stouter runners and larger blossoms, these wildings are said to be one of the ancestors of our domestic berries. Munz says in *A California Flora* that the Chilean form of the species is parental.

I have often accompanied Kathleen Goddard Jones, the "Patron Saint of the Nipomo Dunes," and we have been led to discover these flowers by their fragrance, but I have not found them in fruit on the dunes. I suspect the local wildlife beats us to the small tart-sweet berries. I well remember the taste as a child in Michigan's sand dunes and have found a few in the woods in Monterey County. Trying to think ecologically, it is probably better to take pictures and leave the fruit for the wild creatures. What is a rare treat for us is part of their subsistence and they will distribute the seeds for future plants. Where do the seeds go if we eat them? Into the sewer and oblivion—not a viable ending from the strawberry's point of view!

BEACH MORNING GLORY—*Calystegia soldanella*

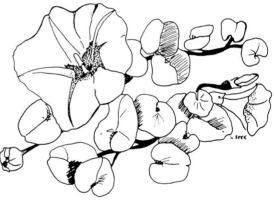

Large distinctive pink and white flowers on a trailing prostrate plant with fleshy green leaves which are often two-lobed at the base. These beautiful beach dwellers belong to a large family, including the white western morning glory that we often see farther inland, and the pestiferous bindweed, but it is the only one found right out in the blowing sand with sea rocket and sand verbena. Beach morning glory's low growth habit, long deep roots, succulent leaves and its tendency to send out runners that help hold it in place while extending new vegetative growth all contribute to its survival where we find it. Look for these hardy perennials April to August. Not limited to the central California coast, beach morning glory grows north to British Columbia and also in South America and many other Pacific seashores. This species, *C. soldanella* (coin-like, referring to the rounded leaves), is distributed along the whole California coast.

BEACH PRIMROSE—*Camissonia* (formerly in *Oenothera*) *cheiranthifolia*

The dime-size bright yellow flowers on this hardy low plant are on several prostrate stems which radiate out from a basal rosette of silvery leaves. The downy foliage helps prevent desiccation and damage by the frequent winds of its habitat.

It truly belongs to the Evening Primrose Family: Onagraceae. Like some other writers, we are dropping the Evening in the common name because its flowers open in the morning and are pollinated by bumblebees who are, of course, active in daylight.

As a docent with the Morro Bay Museum I suppose I've lead perhaps a hundred people in and around the Morro Bay sandspit exploring the dynamics of life in this beautiful but difficult place for plants to live. Wind, blowing abrasive sand, rainwater percolating rapidly down and away from roots are some of the trials. Two pluses are moderate year-round temperatures and fog-drip. There is a fine article in the October 1985 *Fremontia* entitled, "The Morro Bay Sandspit, A California Treasure" by Wayne T. Williams which I have often used on my dune walks and will quote from here because it is pertinent. "...The plant's bright yellow flowers cover new sand deposits everywhere along the sandspit, enhancing dune stability. Its blossoms face downwind. The pollinator is an exceptionally large bumblebee (*Bombus* sp). We have all heard how bumblebees manage to fly despite the aerodynamic engineering theory that would render them land-bound because of their weight and size. These bees deftly approach the beach primrose flowers by flying upwind for greatest flight stability. Their powerful thorax muscles and large size allow them to survive within this niche, gathering food and pollinating, because of the downwind direction of the primrose corollas. Since the primrose is decumbent where wind speed is slowest, the bees can also work over large territories. I have often watched these bees, and have never seen any other species pollinating beach primrose at the sand dunes. This symbiosis between plant and insect allows both the plant and bumblebee to thrive and reproduce...."

SAND PLANT—*Pholisma arenarium*

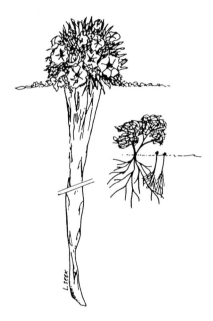

One may find dry brownish "pincushions" in the open sand or under the edge of shrubs on the dunes or further back in coastal scrub any time of year, but in late spring, May and June, we find pretty little pinky-lavender, flaring, tubular flowers with white edges peeking out of the sandy conical mushroom-like "buttons" just above the surface of the sand. A very close look reveals six or seven tightly packed anthers down in the tube. The fleshy whitish stem (of which we see very little) may go down in the sandy soil 18 inches or more, as pholisma is essentially a subterranean parasite on certain soil fungi that are in turn parasitic on the roots of nearby shrubs. Recent studies show that radioactively labeled sugars find their way through this three-way relationship.

Pholisma is a flowering plant, in wet years pushing up the above-ground parts to produce flowers and seeds. Commonly thought to parasitize the roots of mock heather (*Ericamaria ericoides*) and possibly silver lupine, it may be found at the south end of Morro Bay, in the Elfin Forest north of 15th Street in Baywood Park and in the Nipomo Dunes. In future springs let's watch for toadstools near mock heather and pholisma; they may be the spore-bearing fruiting bodies of the intermediate host. There is more to be learned about these strange and fascinating forms of plant life.

GOLDEN YARROW—*Eriophyllum* spp.
WHITE or COMMON YARROW—*Achillea* spp.

Golden Yarrow

Common Yarrow

Dense, bright yellow flower heads occurring in rather flat-topped clusters make golden yarrow a very pretty plant during its blooming time. They begin in April which is early for sunflowers, as many of our coastal kinds don't bloom until August. A sub-shrub two feet to waist high with some white wool underneath (Greek names: erion means wool and phyllum means leaf). Do not be confused by common names. Golden yarrow is in the genus eriophyllum of the Sneezeweed Tribe of the Sunflower Family, while common yarrow is in the genus achillea of the Mayweed Tribe of the same family! When you notice these important differences, you'll not be confused anymore: common yarrow has delicate fern-like leaves and white flowers; golden yarrow has small but coarser, much-divided finger-like leaves and yellow flowers.

In writing this book I'm forced to face up to and cope with a life-long aversion to almost all of the Sunflower Family. However, they are dynamic contributors to the many ecosystems to which they are adapted and very successful reproducers as well as offering easy and handsome members for beginning gardeners.

BLUE LARKSPUR—*Delphinium parryi* ssp. *blochmaniae*

After the abundant March rains in 1991 the Nipomo Dunes put on a truly magnificent display of wildflowers. Coreopsis Hill was golden with its namesake and closer looks revealed rather ghostly tall and softly hairy new larkspur buds and those dainty but colorful carnival poppies, *Meconella linearis*, whose buds are rose-red on the outside, but open alternate yellow and white petals inside. Their slender nodding stems aid this colorful display as they dance in the breezes coming up from the sea. "Like a colorful carnival," said Kathleen Goddard Jones, who gave them their common name.

The larkspur is a lovely light blue when fully open, and possessed of a general covering of soft hairs throughout the plant in its early budding stages. It is one of 30 species state-wide. The showy parts are the calyx, the petals being small and whitish in the center. Larkspur pollinators must push up under the petals, crawl over the stamens and pistil, then reach way down the spur (a modified sepal) to the sweet nectar in its lower tip. *D.p. blochmaniae* is found in Santa Barbara and San Luis Obispo counties. Darker blue forms of *D. parryi* are found both north and south. So we need not worry overmuch about names: larkspurs are a happy element in the spring scene and fulfill their dynamic roles in the natural world regardless of what we call them!

GIANT COREOPSIS—*Coreopsis gigantea*

This plant is a stout, erect, fleshy, few-branched arborescent shrub. Its light green much-divided leaves grow in dense tufts on ends of trunk and branches. The blossoms, with ten to 16 yellow ray flowers around the outside and many tiny yellowish disk flowers in the center, look much like other native annual coreopsis as well as the common garden kinds. All are complete flowers having both stamens (male) and pistils (female).

I admit to a definite bias against composites (*C. gigantea* belongs to the Asteraceae or Sunflower Family, formerly Compositae Family) in general, so they get lumped in my head as D.L.C.s— "Dirty Lousy Composites." However, to this one I bow very low in admiration. To come to the head of a steep rocky canyon clad with them on the Channel Islands off the coast of Santa Barbara County or to plow across the Nipomo Dunes from Oso Flaco Lake

toward Little Coreopsis Hill in San Luis Obispo County at the height of blooming in spring is a heart-warming experience for flower lovers.

I wish I knew more about how they evolved their tall stout angular trunks. That they are brittle and store moisture, I know, because when one gets broken in my garden, the inside is soaking wet even in the depths of summer. (When I first saw them growing at Rancho Santa Ana Botanical Garden they looked to me as though they should have a few young dinosaurs standing among them; there is a primordial aspect to them.)

Coreopsis-like composites in general are highly successful in attracting pollinators. Think like an insect for a minute: how great to land on a sunflower and get many, many sips of nectar by just probing and turning before having to fly again. This works well for the plant, too, in its natural production of seeds.

Why the natural distribution of giant coreopsis is so limited seems strange, as it does well in gardens. My first planting was probably in 1980. Most of these plants in the years since have been replaced by their own naturally occurring seedlings. They may have a longer blooming period here or it just seems so, because they don't all bloom at once. I had flowers in December on a stalk that was beginning its fourth blooming season quite early.

In April of 1991 when it had rained all of March (13-plus inches) after the fifth winter of drought, I helped with the California Native Plant Society Wildflower Weekend at Coreopsis Hill in the Nipomo Dunes. Truly good fortune brought all those flower lovers from all over the state to San Luis Obispo County when the giant coreopsis were at their peak blooming period and carnival poppy—*Meconella linearis,* blue larkspur—*Delphinium parryi* and sand verbena— *Abronia umbellata* were also beginning. It was one of those heady experiences of natural wonder and such fun to share.

3. SEA BLUFFS

CALIFORNIA POPPY—*Eschscholzia californica*

Our state flower, and rightly so, as it's a living symbol of our year-around sunshine and the precious metal that brought the '49ers. This yellow-gold flower enlivens our gardens and roadsides as well as wild places everywhere. Sometimes a single poppy plant will develop a carrot-like root and spread out its foliage over two to three feet of ground, putting out a few flowers as it winters over, then joining the seedlings in a mass of vibrant golden yellow in spring. Such a vigorous plant will even crowd out weeds. Poppies may be seen to respond to changes in sunlight. Bright sun triggers bud opening; when rain clouds reduce the light, the petals serve as raincoats and close around the vital stamens and pistil until the light brightens. Then they open again, ready for the first pollinator to take wing as the temperature rises.

Being aware of this natural phenomenon, you can have a poppy bouquet in the house if you'll go out in your garden (not a wild place, where an arm-of-the-law might pounce upon you!) with a flashlight at night and cut a handful of long-stemmed buds and put them in water. In the morning, they'll be smiling at you and continue thus for four or five days. You can have a handsome centerpiece on your dinner table. A thought for psycho/philosophic types: How do you feel about interrupting the sex life of this very active reproducer? Well, you can set your bouquet out in the garden again. After pollination, the poppy plants will drop the petals and put all their energy into making seeds.

A pioneer plant in disturbed places, poppies have followed two-legged pioneers, especially those with plows, ditch-diggers and bulldozers. One autumn a minor mountain of dirt was stored on a field next to the Rancho Santa Ana Botanic Garden. When spring arrived there were quite a few poppies blooming on the raw soil. The next year it was a mini-mountain of golden poppies. If you have even a tiny native garden, as I do, there will always be a few poppies when there is practically nothing else blooming on your block!

Hooray for California poppies!

SEA DAISY—*Erigeron glaucus*

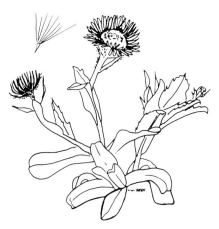

Heads with large lavender-blue ray flowers surrounding broad centers of yellow disk flowers top rosettes of good-sized green leaves on erect or prostrate fleshy and hairy stems in this strictly coastal member of the Sunflower Family. Its Greek name freely means "early-flowering plant with woolly hairs." This hardy perennial is found on the Channel Islands off the shores of Santa Barbara County and north, and they bloom from April to September.

I first found this rugged perennial daisy at Point Lobos State Park on the bluffs of Monterey County. It and various dudleyas were clinging to the lips of those rocky headlands with apparently the same tenacity as mussels and barnacles cling to the intertidal zones below. Sea daisy also happily grows, blooms and spreads in my little native garden, farther back from the sea, but well within the coastal climate.

WILD IRIS or BLUE FLAG—*Iris douglasiana*

Our wildflower belongs to a family of plants that has been widely cultivated around the world for a long time. The family also includes gladiola, crocus, freesia and fleur-de-lis. Since ours was named for David Douglas, an early collector on the west coast, I assume it is a true "wilding," unmanipulated by man until quite recently, when Lee Lenz of Rancho Santa Ana Botanic Garden did careful color selections. Some cultivars are available in the trade and are worth trying in drought tolerant native gardens. Alice

Meyer, number one green thumb in my experience and long time pillar of the San Luis Obispo chapter of the California Native Plant Society has grown wild iris *from seed*. She shared her experience with me. She started her iris seeds in damp peat moss in the least cold area of her refrigerator. She remembers that they were very slow germinating. When they did, she planted them in a south exposure in her garden in Los Osos. For three or four years, she had green leaves without blooms. In the early spring of the fourth or fifth year, Alice tells me that she shook her finger at the iris plants and threatened that she would pull them out if they did not bloom. Voilà—a month later pale blue flowers opened!

Tame or wild iris has evolved a special way of getting pollinated effectively by bees. As you look straight down onto a flower, the first three petals are really modified styles, with the stigma attached on the underside. Pull back the style gently to find it. The true petals are the three reflexed ones underneath. Are you patient enough to watch a field bee push her way down to the nectar? She'll touch both the anthers and the stigma en route. Ideally she brings pollen (from a previous visit to another iris) to the stigma, and takes pollen from these anthers on to the next flower. The sexual parts maturing at different times helps to achieve this ideal! Both wild and honey bees are good cross pollinators, while hummingbirds slip their long thin bills in for a sweet sip, without coming in contact with the flowers' sexual parts. However, hummers may earn their interdependent service-stripes at flowers that have evolved for their kind of services. Examples are scarlet bugler and climbing penstemon.

BLUFF GILIA or FRINGED PHLOX—*Linanthus* spp.

Our local five-petaled pretties have tiny teeth on the outer edge, and run the color spectrum from pink through lavender to white. They are a close relative of gilias in the phlox family. Walking the bluffs on a pleasant day as early as January, you'll be happy, I think, to find these slender stemmed wildflowers growing close to the ground in open sandy places. Illustrated is *L. grandiflorus.*

BLUE DICKS or BRODIAEA—*Dichelostemma pulchella*

These blue-violet members of the Amaryllis Family have dense heads of individual flowers on a long naked stem. When fall rains are good and well spaced, two strap-like leaves first appear above ground; one is usually broader than the other. They rise from a small white bulb in a brown skin-like wrapper. If the bulb is young it will send up leaves only, manufacturing food in sunlight and storing it in the bulb for several years. When it is mature enough to spend the extra energy needed for reproduction, it will send up a stalk and bloom. In dry years, we see few or no blossoms in familiar places. They have not died, but only lie in the ground waiting for the right conditions to come again. Widely distributed in our area, blue dicks are, to me, as much a part of California spring as poppies. Their colors often complement each other on grassy slopes.

After World War II, my spouse and I "homesteaded" ten acres in the back country of southern California. We worked intermittently at hand-digging a fair sized hole on the side of the hill behind the slowly rising house. The soil was heavy clay and disintegrated granite. We'd pour water in and come back hours later when it had soaked in to dig out a couple of buckets of dirt and add more water. I had a real surprise one day when I found in the steep wall a little bulb. I carefully scratched it out and showed it to Murray. He measured the depth from ground surface to the bulb's site: 25 inches! We replanted it above the dry rock wall in front of the house, where it grew and bloomed. Our first step into a long, happy experience of gardening with native plants.

SEA THRIFT or SEA PINK—*Armeria maritima* var. *californica*

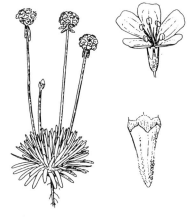

Globe-shaped heads of pretty rose-pink flowers, densely packed together above various papery bracts atop long naked stems rising out of a bunch of narrow persistent basal leaves; this is sea thrift. A happy find in late spring along low grassy bluffs in San Luis Obispo County and northward, sea thrift is not as common as it used to be. A perennial herb with five petals and stamens, it is related to marsh rose-mary in the Leadwort Family. Another relative (I don't know its correct name, but I call it "moss pink") is common and attractive in gardens, being bright green bunches topped with shorter and more numerous pink flowers. In my little native garden I have a lusty sea thrift which I brought home from that wonderful Yerba Buena Nursery in Woodside in San Mateo County. I made a small but interesting discovery with my hand lens. The flowers around the outside of the head have several bright green anthers on the stamens, while the center flowers show yellow pollen on all five stamens or nothing but the whitish filament. Are the green anthers new unopened ones? Sometimes the more you see the less you know! If anyone has clues to my mystery, please drop me a note via the publisher.

FOOTSTEPS OF SPRING—*Sanicula arctopoides*

These low clusters of tiny yellow flowers radiate above a mat of prickly-looking, yellow-green leaves which are much divided; they are members of the Parsley Family which also includes dill, caraway and poison hemlock.

One February, starting up the high trail at Garapata State Park south of Yankee Point in Monterey County, we came across scattered "footsteps" (the species name means "bear's foot" in Greek) dimpling the short grass. That March we found it again on the grassy bluff at San Simeon in San Luis Obispo County, so these two discoveries certainly document the validity of the common name for this winsome harbinger of spring.

LIVE-FOREVER—*Dudleya* spp.

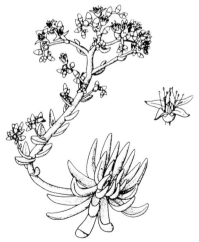

Other common names for members of this interesting genus are sea lettuce, rock lettuce, chalk dudleya and hen-and-chicks. The fleshy green leaves grow in handsome rosettes often with reddish tips and/or edges and usually with a fine whitish coating. In spring they send up a fairly stout flower stalk on which rosy buds develop. These in time open to reveal yellow petals, though the color varies from pale yellow to orange-red. On some dudleyas the flower heads nod.

It is not difficult to guess how the name "live-forever" came into use. I've found little wizened-up gray rosettes in rock crevices and assumed they were dead plants, only to come by after rain or even a period of foggy weather and, lo and behold, the same rosette is plump and green and starting to send up a flower or add another chick. They have tremendous ability to store moisture and survive long periods of drought.

Dudleyas occupy a diverse assortment of habitats from sea stacks, the precarious lip of bluffs, scrub, shaded banks and grassland hilltops, to rocky cliffs and canyon walls. Recently we found old plants with very long stems trailing down above the entrance to the manmade tunnel at Partington Cove in Julia Pfeiffer Burns State Park in Monterey County. They take the prize in my experience for cliff-hanging plants!

CHECKER BLOOM or WILD HOLLYHOCK— *Sidalcea malvaeflora*

The rose to pink flowers of this member of the Mallow Family is a delight to find in spring, blowing in the breezes on grassy bluffs along the coast and in damp grassy places inland as well, from southern Oregon to the Mexican border. Though rather variable in color and form, checker bloom is a perennial plant with spreading root stocks and stems, one-half to two feet tall. Looking into a flower we usually find the stamens forming a tube around the wispy styles. Our species has entire basal leaves, while those on the stem are deeply lobed. I first found these floral lovelies

near a lighthouse, dancing in the wind, but have since found them on grassy banks along the back country roads of Santa Barbara and San Luis Obispo counties. It is here that they remind me most of their domestic cousins, the hollyhocks.

REIN ORCHID—*Habenaria elegans*

It's a happy surprise to come upon these delicate lovelies. We have found them on the sea bluffs, up on a knob 200 feet above Islay Creek and beside a pile of dead brush by a trail midway between the previous elevations, all in Montaña de Oro State Park, San Luis Obispo County. C.F. Smith has reported them in-

land and up on Figueroa Mountain in Santa Barbara County while P.A. Munz has them in Monterey County and north (see Further Reading List for references).

The dense spikes with greenish-white flowers grow to 16 inches high. Each small flower has a spur going fairly straight down a half inch or more. It blooms from July to September. Rein orchid and other orchids, as well as lilies, have leaves with parallel veins and flower parts in threes.

MEXICAN SAGE—*Salvia greggii*

Perhaps the showiest of our local sages is this half shrub (woody base with herbaceous top) which has bright red flowers scattered over it in autumn. Another lip-shaped mint, the exaggerated banner is a four-scalloped smooth petal, while the smaller upright keel is covered with fine fuzz. The flower tube is encased in the calyx, and shows faint white in the throat. A profile view reveals the two unequal stigma forks protruding slightly over the tip of the keel. A closer look inside the keel shows yellow pollen still in closed anthers.

So we probably have here an example of a "first female" flower; i.e. the stigma receives pollen brought by a pollinator from another flower before these anthers are mature, assuring cross pollination. I made this interesting discovery in my own front yard where a Mexican sage grows beside a rain barrel under a downspout from the house eaves. It probably gets a little extra of the lovely soft rainwater as I carry gallon scoops around to other plants in my little native garden. Consequently it has a few saucy red-lipped blooms on it almost year-around.

This cultivar was collected in Saltillo, Mexico, by Dr. Josiah Gregg. The word cultivar refers to "a variety that has originated and persisted under cultivation, not necessarily referable to a botanical species," according to L.H. Bailey, which means that the variety may be a cross of two or more species. I brought mine home from a California Native Plant Society plant sale in San Luis Obispo several years ago. It gets leggy so must be pruned back occasionally. From the pruning tips I often get a nosegay to put in water on a table in the house. It roots readily from runners. Mexican sage is popular with hummingbirds.

Little leaf sage—*S. microphylla*—is a similar plant which is also cultivated for ornamental horticulture.

SENECIO (also called GROUNDSEL or RAGWORT)—*Senecio* spp.

Our drawing is *S. californicus*, an annual species one to one and a half feet high with heads plus or minus one inch across. These yellow sunflowers are found in dry open places from Monterey and Tulare Counties south. Probably we can save ourselves some frustration by simply calling these cheery flowers senecio, which has a nice ring to it, I think. You will note that the flower heads are a much looser cluster 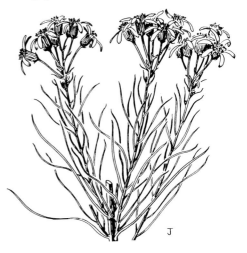 than those of golden yarrow, but they are true composites.

On each head the outer flowers are petal-like and are called ray flowers (usually one large ray petal per flower) and are generally imperfect. The inner flowers are tubular and do not appear to us to have petals; they are called disk flowers. The important thing to remember is that disk flowers usually have both sexual elements and, as perfect flowers, are therefore capable of making seeds. There is an infinite variety of sunflowers; the genus senecio, for example, has over a thousand species, many without common names. So don't worry if the pictured leaves aren't just like the one on "your" flower. Botanists don't seem to classify sunflowers by gross characteristics that we can readily see; they use words like "pappus, involucrate and phyllary"—a technical language beyond the scope of this book. I hope we can give you clues and pictures that will help you enjoy our commonly found winsome genera like senecio.

BLUE-EYED GRASS—*Sisyrinchium bellum*

These pert purple flowers are not grass, of course, but they are in the Iris Family as you can see by the way the flower stalk rises up through the folded linear leaves just as tame iris does. Unlike wild iris though they are vigorous seed and new plant makers. I brought a gallon can home from a local Native Plant Society sale and set it out in a window box where it flourished and was pleasing to enjoy from inside as well as outside. Also the next year little blue-eyed grass plants showed up down in the garden. One has to be careful not to pull up these seedlings with the weeds as they do resemble grass superficially. Some of those "jumped down" plants bloomed that second year. The three sepals and three petals (look-alikes) each have a bright yellow nectar guide at the petal base. I've yet to spy a pollinator in the act, though I live in hope!

Blue-eyed grass is found in moist places at low elevations in all three of the central coast counties and north. They are also plentiful in years of good rainfall east of the Salinas River. A less common species is *S. californicus* or golden-eyed grass which occurs along the coast from Piedras Blancas Point northward.

4. COASTAL SCRUB

OWL'S CLOVER—*Orthocarpus purpurascens*

These are low erect annuals (from seed) whose terminal spikes consist of plump pinkish-red flowers all mixed in with variable purplish bracts. The leaves are alternate and usually deeply lobed. Each corolla has a short stubby upper lip and a large lower lip with pouches. Some flowers are whitish-pink with dark "eye spots."

Folks sometimes confuse Johnny Tuck—*O. erianthus*—also called butter-and-eggs, with owl's clover. Four to 12 inches tall, Johnny Tuck's corolla has a small upper lip, but the lower lip is three inflated pouches. There are bracts below the flowers, but the pouches stand way out from them. Yellow and white flowers are called butter-and-eggs; pink and white ones, Johnny Tuck. These are handsome flowers, but not to be confused with owl's clover. During the El Niño years (1982 and 1983), Johnny Tucks were rampant in the scrub near Shark Inlet of Morro Bay and in 1991, after the marvelous March rains, we found great splashes of them on west facing slopes above small creeks on the eastern side of Ventana Wilderness in Monterey County.

There is also Johnny Nip—*O. castillejoides*—the paintbrush-like owl's clover that grows in saline places and sea bluffs, such as the sea bluffs in Cambria, San Luis Obispo County. "Nip and Tuck" may throw some light on the common names, but who was Johnny?

If nostalgia bores you, turn the page, but some of you will remember springs when many southern Californians made all-day pilgrimages with a picnic and a collection of Richfield Flower booklets over the "Ridge Route" (with a pause on top to let the radiator stop boiling, so some water could be added to the stressed car.) Then down below into the valley all blue and gold, from Grapevine to Arvin we went through ever-expanding fields of wildflowers. I was often delegated to spread the red-checked picnic cloth where it would not crush flowers. Impossible! Cars had running boards then and that is where the picnic was spread. In those fields near Bakersfield is where I first found owl's clover. So there

I returned years later with my first close-up lens. Eventually I got a slide of one owl's clover inflorescence with ten owls looking right back at me from the projection screen and we knew the reason for the common name. That same trip I also got one of a friend down on her hunkers with her hand lens looking into owl's eyes. She was surrounded by miles, it seemed, of rosy red and soft greens on the hills. Owl's clovers still do this for us in springs when natural conditions are right and we and our high-tech agriculture leave them space to do it.

STAR LILY—*Zigadenus fremontii*

A harbinger of spring, these greenish-white six-parted flowers rise rapidly from their green parallel-veined leaves that emerge from a bulb in the rain-softened earth as daylight begins to lengthen. Good-sized heads of blossoms peek out from under shrubs along hilly trails or dance together in large numbers in breezy, moist valleys in March.

I have found very vigorous plants coming up among blackened stalks after a brush fire, perhaps benefiting from nutrients returned to the soil in the ash, as well as getting more sunlight. These lilies grow as far east as the La Panza Range.

DEERWEED—*Lotus scoparius*

This bushy green member of the Pea Family has a long blooming period in wet years, beginning in March and lasting all summer, where they are festooned with masses of small yellow "sweet peas." The three leaflets are about one half inch long and flowers come out of the leaf axils. The corolla is usually one third of an inch long, bright yellow, sometimes tinged with red or orange on bud tips and the back of the banner. Deerweed attracts butterflies, bees and other small pollinators and they set many seeds in fat little green seed pods. They are also "popular" with small herbivores (as well as deer) including the endangered Morro

Bay kangaroo rats who eat seeds, stems and leaves and store many seeds in their underground granaries.

Dr. Aryan Roest and Dr. Roger Gambs and their Cal Poly students, California Department of Fish and Game, and California Department of Parks and Recreation, all separately and together have for many years attempted to improve survival conditions for the kangaroo rats in the northern part of Montaña de Oro State Park. Before this park was established, part of this area was used by the military during World War II and was then scraped bare of all vegetation. In the fifty years since that war, it has been a prime place for observing natural regeneration. Deerweed was an early comer in this area and is still abundant, though with time these pioneer plants generally get crowded out by the slower growing woody-based shrubs like mock heather, black sage, buckwheat and California sagebrush. So while you are wandering among the flowers in this rich scrub area, remember to watch for the tail-drag marks with footprints in the sand and the arched burrow entrances (plugged) of this large eyed, nocturnal creature who may be for us what the canary in the mine shaft was for earlier day miners.

AMOLE or SOAP PLANT—*Chlorogalum pomeridianum*

Early in spring, the long green wavy-edged leaves help us distinguish young amole plants from other lilies. Soap plant's small white flowers open in late afternoon. If visited by nocturnal pollinators, these flowers will wither and the energy go to devel-

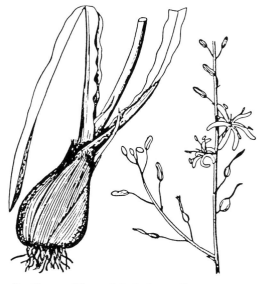

oping seed. New flowers up the tall, slender, much-branched stems will open in the dusky low light of June evenings. My flashlight has caught the tiny shine of nectar, but not yet a pollinator.

Amole concentrates saponins from the soil in its underground bulb. Saponins form a soapy foam when dissolved in water. Native Americans knew the right time to dig them. They dried them for many uses and trade.

Indians and early settlers used amole in the place of soap. The inner bulb was crushed and rubbed on hands or clothes or hair in water, making a good lather. Lacking alkali, no "conditioner" rinse following shampoo was necessary.

Fish were temporarily stupefied and caught by adding crushed bulbs to dammed up creeks. A whole village worked together, bringing rocks for the dam, gathering and crushing amole and collecting the stupefied fish to clean, smoke and dry. This stunning of the fish did not affect their food value and no ill effects have ever been reported from eating fish so caught. This method of gathering fish for food is known to the natives in other parts of the world who use other plants with similar properties.

Some California tribes used amole for food, baking the bulbs in a stone-lined pit overnight. The slow baking destroyed the saponins, leaving good nourishment.

The Miwoks and other California Natives made useful brushes out of the brown fibrous wrappers that grow around the outside of the bulb. They coated the brush handle with a glue made by boiling up the inner part. I have long admired artifact soap plant brushes in museums and hence was delighted to make one myself under the direction of Dorothy Stanley, a Sierra Miwok.

SAGES—*Salvia* spp.

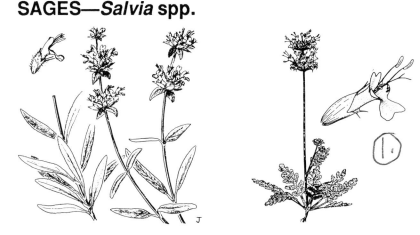

Black Sage   *Chia*

Our three counties on the central coast are rich in handsome members of the salvia genus and close cousins. All have aromatic foliage, are useful for seasoning drinks or stews, and show their membership in the Mint Family by having square stems. Most produce their lip-shaped flowers and tiny nutrient-packed seeds in conspicuous buttons which rise on slender stems above the bush or basal rosette of leaves.

> Please note: These sages are members of the Mint Family known as the "true sages," not to be confused with the sagebrushes, which are also aromatic, but belong to the Sunflower Family. Common examples of the latter are California sagebrush—*Artemisia californica*—and Great Basin sagebrush—*A. tridentata*. Sagebrushes are not included in this book due to less than eye-catching flowers. California sagebrush is an important element in the Coastal Scrub in much of our area, however.

BLACK SAGE—*Salvia mellifera*—is a small but ubiquitous shrub. With coyote bush, California sagebrush, bush monkeyflower and others, it makes up the coastal scrub plant community which once covered a great deal of the central coast's low rolling hills, now occupied by our towns, farms and cattle-grazing ranches. Still widespread on higher, rockier slopes, it has numerous tiny white to lavender flowers which bloom for four to six weeks, offering many sweet sips to numerous tiny insects as well as honey bees.

CHIA—*Salvia columbariae*—is a herbaceous blue-flowered sage which is small but widespread in wet years when many buttons develop up its slender stems. In dry years, a plant may pro-

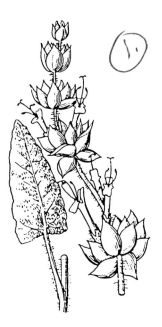

Hummingbird Sage

duce only one short stem with one or two buttons. But flowers grow, get pollinated and seed is set by this handsome hardy survivor. The plentiful seeds were important to Native Americans who recognized their nutrient value and carried them on long journeys.

HUMMINGBIRD SAGE—*Salvia spathacea*—has red flowers which make it popular with its feathered namesake. This large-leafed, coarse-foliaged plant associates with black sage and bush monkeyflowers in the coastal scrub and may also be found under trees in foothill woodland. Useful in gardens, it reproduces by underground runners as well as seeds. With a light monthly watering, it will continue to flower almost all year around.

SUNCUPS—*Camissonia* (formerly *Oenothera*) *bistorta*

This pretty yellow annual may begin to bloom in January. The four petals, more or less a half inch long, often have a dark spot near each base, which may be a nectar guide for pollinators. The flowers have a short tube and grow in the axils of the well-developed leaves. Usually only a few flowers bloom at a time per plant, and they open in sunshine even though they belong to the Evening Primrose Family. The stamens are unequal in length and the stigma is a rounded knob. The seed pods are twisted or contorted. After a wet winter these flowers sprinkle sunshine among the drab bushes in sandy scrub fields of the coastal areas of our three counties. Our drawing is of a closely related species, *C. ovata.*

YERBA SANTA—*Eriodictyon* spp.

Greek name: erion = wool and diktuon = net, describing the underside of the leaves. Our color photograph is of *E. tomentosum* (page C-20) which is covered throughout with a thick white to olive-green felt (use your hand lens!). Our drawing is *E. californicum.* I use the common name for the whole genus, preferring to consider their marvelous survival adaptations rather than minute structures with multitudinous and difficult names. Yerba santas are evergreen aromatic shrubs, with shedding bark and an open growth habit from woody underground rootstocks. Leaves are sticky and shallowly toothed. Flowers are many in branched, coiled clusters. Blooming from May to July, corollas are white to lavender and tubular. Seeds are small and numerous, but I suspect those root runners do most of the reproduction.

Yerba santa is a special plant to me partly due to its aroma and flowers and also because I first discovered it after an extensive brush fire in southern California. I'd just been studying about the ecology of fire in summer school and there it was doing it! Living up here and exploring in "east county," I've again found it growing with vigor after the various Las Pilitas fires. I have also found it in the Arroyo Seco area of Monterey County and the Santa Ynez Mountains of Santa Barbara County though not so obviously associated with fire. Yerba santa is a fairly short-lived shrub that gets crowded out after several years by slower growing longer-lived shrubs. But soon after the dry rocky hillsides are cleared by fire, it takes its place in sunlight, uses some of the nutrients from the ash incorporated into the soil and grows lustily and flowers handsomely.

Yerba santa—"saintly herb"—was used by Native Americans and early settlers as a remedy for colds, asthma, etc.

WILD ROSE—*Rosa californica*

Roses have been selected, hybridized, named, patented and shown competitively. All in one way or another satisfies man's compelling need to improve on natural beauty. To each his own; for me there is nothing better than coming upon a basic wild rose with five, pink, satin-smooth petals surrounding many yellow stamens and a cluster of paler yellow pistils in the middle. If my nose catches the wonderful fragrance before I see the flower, so much the better. It's a really good thing our needs are not all the same! The Rose Family also has in it apples, pears, apricots, plums, strawberries and raspberries.

In June, 1991, I found low growing rose bushes blooming atop Black Hill here in Morro Bay, where I've never seen them before. We also commonly find them making dense thickets three and four feet high along Shark Inlet at the south end of Morro Bay. Our California wild rose has recurved prickles and smooth-edged green sepals which separates it from more northern wild roses. In late summer we begin to find the red hips or seedpods which are loaded with vitamin C. Actually rose hips are reported to contain more vitamin C, calcium, phosphorus and iron than oranges. Hips can be dried for tea or used to make jelly. The dry inner seeds should be removed. The hips remain on the bushes through the winter providing good forage for wildlife as long as they last. Rose thickets offer shelter for small mammals and nesting sites for birds. Natural rose thickets have long been augmented by planting along dikes in wildlife refuges on bird migration flyways.

ROSE MALLOW—*Lavatera assurgentiflora*

This erect, rapid growing softwood evergreen shrub grows to fifteen feet tall. The light green leaves are five-lobed, up to five inches across, smooth on top, soft and silvery underneath. The very attractive flowers are two inches across, rose violet with light centers and purple striping. The flower has five petals and a prominent cylinder of light colored stamens. When the anthers have shed their pollen and wilted, the long slender purple stigmas become conspicuous at the top of the cylinder. The one inch or more flower stems flex this way and that—perhaps to let the flowers peek out from under the very large leaves. The green seed pods look like the little hollyhock "cheeses" we played with as kids.

Rose mallow has long been in cultivation in California and many volunteers grace vacant weed lots in our area. It is useful as a fast growing hedge in coastal areas as it's resistant to both wind and salt spray. It must be sheared several times a year to keep it dense and attractive. Difficult and fleeting as a cut flower, I sometimes float the flowers in a brandy snifter. A few flowers are available from yard shrubs year around.

The Mallow Family is mostly Mediterranean but this lavatera is native to the Channel Islands off the coast of Santa Barbara. It is purported to be the living shrub that helped support the driftwood house of the Chumash woman who lived alone on San Nicholas Island for 16 years. The *Island of the Blue Dolphin* is a fictionalized book based on her real life experience. Rose mallow is also called California tree mallow, though 15 feet high does not make a tree in my book!

POISON OAK—*Toxicodendron diversilobum*

Ubiquitous in most of our area, it climbs trees like a vine, makes bushy thickets of flexible wands and produces in the fall the west's best flaming red leaves.

"Leaves of three, let it be," the age old jingle, is still the best advice to refrain from getting the skin rash it may cause. Also wear long sleeves, slacks and gloves when exploring in wild places. Most people must physically brush against a plant, leaves or bare winter stems to be affected. A very few people get the rash from petting dogs or handling clothing that have been out in it. Some

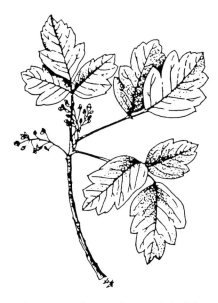

people seem to be immune to the toxin which exudes as a volatile oil from the breathing pores on most parts of the plant, though there is documented evidence that this immunity can change, even after many years. Hikers and forest fire fighters, who naturally perspire freely, are vulnerable as the chemistry happens most readily when the toxin is brushed on warm, moist skin.

Youth group leaders who brought their children to the botanic garden where I worked as a guide, expressly to imprint them about this "dangerous" plant, brought out the "Pollyanna" in me! As we continued our walk around the large sylvan acreage of "undangerous" plants, I tried to draw from the children, with questions, the many positive values of poison oak in the larger than one-on-one dynamics of the living world. The kids often did well, thinking of "good things" about poison oak: makes berries for birds to eat, provides nectar for bees, provides hiding places for quail and bunny rabbits; like all green plants, it uses carbon dioxide and produces oxygen on which we depend; dead leaves, etc., feed the decay organisms helping to enrich the soil. Being small humanistic people, they sometimes mentioned, "pretty in autumn" and "keeps people on the paths." Our 90-acre Los Osos Oaks State Reserve is a good example of this last one; the handsome, gnarled old trees have an almost continuous groundcover of poison oak.

I have never heard of anyone dying of poison oak; a week with a few patches of blisters may be worth the grand experience of a lovely walk in beautiful woods to some; if not to you, go to the beach! There are excellent palliatives available today. It grieves me to hear people on my museum walks "decide" that they are "very allergic" to poison oak without really knowing.

CHOCOLATE LILY or CHECKER LILY or MISSION BELLS—*Calochortus* spp.

It's always a happy surprise to come upon these handsome, nodding, bell-shaped flowers in spring in the scrub or sparse chaparral or along a wood's edge. I have found colors ranging from greenish-brown through dark purple to brown, yes chocolate brown. You may be reasonably sure you are looking at a calochortus if its leaves are mostly basal, broad and pointed; the flowers nod and the style is three parted.

WILD CUCUMBER—*Marah fabaceus*

This native vine is a special plant for me. We "homesteaded" ten acres of brush after World War II. We found a pack rat also in residence on "our" property. He was the first neighbor with whom we became acquainted. We noticed pieces of the large cucumber pods on his brush pile home and wondered what he saw in them and thus on our rambling walks got to watching the growth and development of cuke plants. They grow rapidly after sufficient winter rains. First come the exploring shoots, then the attractive leaves and tendrils that wrap around anything that gets the vine up above the bushes and into the sunlight. Then from a leaf axil sprout two to three inch spikes of cheery greenish-white flowers. Then the cukes begin, also at a leaf axil. They grow more slowly but can easily get to be two to three inches long, covered at first with soft green prickles. As spring moves into summer, the warmth of the longer days helps mature the heavy seed pods, and dry the prickles into formidable armor. When ripe, the tips of the pod sections open and curl back and the first big olive-green seeds fall out. We took a few home, but when we passed that vine again the whole pod was gone. We hurried to Mr. Pack Rat's home and there were indeed pod scrapes all about the nest and a length of wilting vine even trailed over the top. Wild cukes were the first plants that I discovered had separate sex flowers on the same plant (monoecious). If you keep looking carefully in the leaf axils below spikes of male flowers, you will eventually find a little whitish flower on its own short stem. Carefully turn the vine so you can see under the petals and there is the fuzzy green ovary that will grow into the large and well defined cuke seed pod.

How Mr. Pack Rat gets past the prickles or opens the big hard seeds, we never discovered. But we did read that wild cucumbers often have a large underground tuber, their "insurance" against drought.

CALIFORNIA FUCHSIA—*Epilobium canum* spp. *mexicanum* (formerly *Zauschneria californica*)

These brilliant scarlet somewhat fuchsia-like flowers are low perennials. The foliage is narrow, gray-green and slightly hairy. The lovely flower is a bit more sophisticated than it looks at first glance. The scarlet calyx is bulged at the base, funnel-form and four-lobed above. The petals, also scarlet, are inserted on the throat of the calyx, alternately with and a little longer than its lobes. The eight stamens stick out the top of the whole flower as does the knobbed stigma. The capsule is four-valved with many seeds.

California fuchsia grows on dry rocky hillsides near the coast in all three counties and on the Channel Islands.

Other similar species grow inland and at higher elevations. In gardens, these plants grow to one or two feet high, the stems branched, some recumbent, others almost erect. Popular with hummingbirds, California fuchsia starts blooming when the last summer beauties have gone by, and blooms profusely on into late fall. It makes a very satisfactory border above the retaining wall in my native garden. It needs to be cut back and thinned at least once a year.

FILAREE or STORKBILL—*Erodium cicutarium*

This rose-lavender flower, a member of the Geranium Family, has five sepals, petals, stamens and a five-parted ovary. The leaves are much divided and make a pretty green rosette on the ground with clusters of pinkish flowers nestled in them. In years of poor winter rains that is about all that happens. But after good wet winters this plant grows vigorously, making extensive, dense stands 18 to 20 inches high. Filaree is reputed to be nutritionally comparable to alfalfa and may have been introduced for pasture enhancement. A European annual, it became widely naturalized in California with the coming of the covered wagons, and still is important forage for sheep and cattle. Filaree's fruits or storksbills are intriguing indeed. After the styles elongate, the developing seeds separate as they dry and corkscrew upward and off (to catch rides on cattle or your socks!) and even help drill their seed into the ground, planting them. We did some fun play-research with filaree seeds at Brownie Day Camp long ago. Hint: Changes in air moisture causes the corkscrewed styles to slowly curl and uncurl. Additional discoveries await patient observers with longer interest spans!

Soon after its introduction, Native Americans were quick to recognize filaree's food value. They gathered the young plants and cooked them or ate them raw, as we can too. C.B. Clarke gives an intriguing recipe for "Filaree Frittata" (see Further Reading List).

Quail, finches, ground squirrels and kangaroo rats have learned to relish this pretty little naturalized citizen.

TOADFLAX—*Linaria* spp.

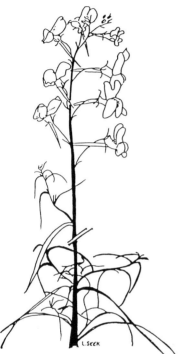

We are including this wild-flower-seed-package plant, naturalized in North America from Europe and North Africa, because you flower lovers will find it along fences, roadsides and in vacant lots as I did, and also because it's such a pretty little "snapdragon." Both Bailey and Hoover include a few linarias and the former authority calls a yellow one, butter-and-eggs—*Linaria vulgaris*. Toadflax runs the gamut of colors from white to purple with rosy-reds and pale to deep yellows. The corolla is two-lipped, the lower lip having a rounded prominence which nearly closes the throat and a long slender spur curving down below it. The upper lip is one cleft petal about as tall as the spur is long. This spur is so slender it hardly looks like it could hold much nectar, but it is in the right position for a pollinator to land on the lower lip and push down past the stamens and pistil and reach into it. Another good chance to laze away some happy time watching to see for yourself how it happens. These lovely little linarias are in riotous bloom in my window box as I write. This spring I found the little "wild" ones blooming along the northwest edges of Morro Bay State Park. They were blue only, with rather abbreviated lip petals, but with good slender spurs perhaps longer than the petals above.

MOCK HEATHER—*Ericameria ericoides*

L. SEEK

This is a compact but spreading heather-like shrub to four feet high. Tops of the bushes are often flat and densely twiggy. The dark leaves with a groove on the back are not more than one-half inch long. They are needle-like and resinous with secondary leaves in the axils. Mock heather's flower heads are yellow and branched. Each head has two to six ray flowers and eight to 12 disk flowers. They are quite showy when they bloom in August through November and may be found on sandy flats and in some places actually on the dunes (as on the Morro Bay sandspit), never far from the sea. In the protected area behind dunes we find a great increase in plant diversity and in plant cover. Three plants are basic to these areas: coyote bush, mock heather and silver lupine. In several ways they make it possible for perennial herbs to grow here. Examples are coast dandelion, agoseris, and cirsium, the beautiful cobwebby native thistle with the soft rose flowers rising out of its "wonderfully-patterned, spirally-arranged spine-tipped bracts," according to Munz. Horticulturally, this evergreen autumn-blooming mock heather is suitable for soil and dune stabilization. The lower portions endure much submergence by sand and the wind-pruned upper parts provide protection on the lee side for other more delicate plants. Mock heather is a member of the Sunflower Family and is thought to be one of the major hosts for pholisma or sandplant.

BUSH or STICKY MONKEY FLOWER—
Mimulus aurantiacus

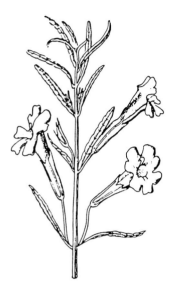

Blooming bush monkey flower and black sage are the spring garments on our rocky hillsides every year and this one keeps on blooming for three or four months, from April on usually. Sticky monkey flower is an evergreen, spreading, woody-based shrub up to four feet high. Belonging to the Figwort Family, the stems, leaf undersides and calyxes are quite hairy and viscid. The top side of the leaves are green with rolled edges and the veins visibly impressed. The wonderful flowers are deep apricot to yellow-orange and two inches long. The green calyx has five ribs and makes a sleeve almost an inch long around the corolla. The five stamens and pistil cluster in the top of the flower's throat. The pistil doesn't mature until after the anthers have shed their pollen and withered. Sixth graders touring the Rancho Santa Ana Botanic Garden enjoyed finding receptive stigmas to touch with a pine needle and watching the two lobes close. Returning a while later, they'd find the lobes open again assuring them that you can't fool a monkey flower with your monkeying around!

Bush monkey flowers are valuable garden plants and some interesting colors have been developed by plant breeders. Probably well established shrubs should be cut back after blooming is finished. Water should be withheld during late summer when they are dormant in nature.

STICKY PHACELIA—*Phacelia viscida*

I found this particular phacelia for the first time in early May of 1991 in the Islay Creek area of Montaña de Oro State Park and what a happy discovery it was. This strikingly beautiful flower, with deep blue, open-belled corollas up to one inch across, has five petals, sepals and stamens, the latter with conspicuous round white anthers on top. Look a bit closer and you'll find in the bottom of the open bell a white area surrounded by lavender and white "lace." With many phacelias, the whole plant is hairy or bristly; ours has soft hairs which are only sticky, indicating the accuracy of the common name. Another thing worth noting about phacelias is how the often crowded flower clusters grow on coiled cymes with the central or top flowers opening first. For instance, if your plant has been blooming a while when you discover it, it will have

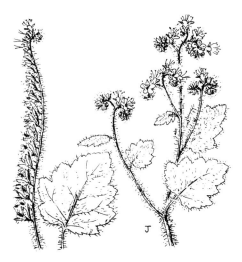

dried up flowers or seed pods *below* the wide open flowers on the one-sided coil, and buds swelling below the open ones. Our drawing is of a related species, stinging phacelia—*P. malvifolia* which also occurs in our area on back beaches and is often called wild heliotrope.

GOLDENROD—*Solidago occidentalis*

Western goldenrod has simple stems which branch near the top, each branch ending in rather rounded clusters of small heads of bright yellow flowers. These heads tend to have many short ray flowers and fewer disk flowers, as contrasted with the common garden sunflower we all know, which has a large area of disk flowers in the middle with fewer ray flowers around the outside edge of the head. These perennial herbs have lance-linear two to four inches long leaves. Like some other coastal scrub dwellers, goldenrod may let its leaves curl and drop off in drought periods to reduce water loss and use energy thus saved for blooming which is typically July through November, long after the rains have ceased. The dried leaves and flowers of goldenrod can be used for tea or as a source of yellow dye. From the *Pharmacopoeia*: the plant produces an astringent which causes tissues to contract and stop bleeding; also it is a diuretic, increasing perspiration.

Like most members of the Sunflower Family there are many, many solidagos. We chose one that is widespread along the California coast.

WOOLLY STAR or ERIASTRUM—*Eriastrum densifolium*

A bit late in spring, it's such a happy surprise to come across clumps of these blue lovelies among sandy openings in the drab coastal scrub. The plants are seldom more than a foot high, the dense clusters of five-petaled tubular flowers are undergirt with unequal calyx lobes and lots of linear leaves. One of the first places I found eriastrum was in El Moro Elfin Forest, in the sandy scrub south of the famous little oaks in Los Osos. The *Floras* indicate that it lives in all three of the counties we chose to cover in this book, Santa Barbara, San Luis Obispo and Monterey.

One June a friend from Claremont paused on his way north and we hiked Montaña de Oro State Park from Hazard Canyon south to Spooner's Cove along the bluff and through the scrub. I'd found eriastrum here previously, but this time they were almost all gone to seed. We gathered a small paper bag of the leafy heads to try to grow the seeds. Alas, they did not germinate. If anyone has grown them successfully from seed, we'd love to hear from you.

INDIAN PINK—*Silene* spp.

Dependably bright red (not the color pink) the common name stems from the fact it is botanically a member of the Pink Family. As I write about this tubular, turned back, fringe-petaled spring wildflower, I see it in my mind's eye peeking out of the scrub east of Shark Inlet at the southern tip of Morro Bay, its bright redness cheering up (for us) the sometimes drab sages, coy-

ote brush and buckwheat. Indian pink is not confined to the scrub, however. Several species are to be found in other plant communities in our three counties. As you probably guessed, it's a popular flower with hummingbirds. It was reportedly used as a tea in pioneer days for aches, sprains and sores.

The petals of this flower are not fused into a tube. Take one apart carefully, if there are plenty growing there to re-seed, and you'll see that the lower part of each petal is confined within a tubular calyx the way a garden bouquet's stems fit down into a bud vase.

PEONY, CALIFORNIA or WILD—*Paeonia californica*

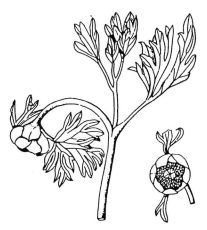

These seemingly shy flowers are an inch or more across and drooping. Their five to ten dark red petals are thick and curved inward and are surrounded by five green persistent sepals. Inside are many stamens and two to five pistils which are on a fleshy base. The pistils produce large fleshy seed pods which open spontaneously when mature to discharge their large red-brown seeds. The gray-green stems with large green leaves divided into three parts grow to sixteen inches high. These atypical scrub plants have deep-seated heavy roots and are perennials, blooming January to April. They occur below 4000 feet in open brush, usually back from the sea a half mile or more, and are found in Monterey County and south in the Coast Ranges and eastward to the La Panza Range.

The Greek name paeonia is derived from *Peon*, who was the

physician of the gods, and early Californians considered the fleshy root a remedy for dyspepsia if eaten raw. There are about 30 species in the northern hemisphere, largely Asian; many have horticultural value.

WILD BUCKWHEAT—*Eriogonum parvifolium*

Wild buckwheat is such an important element in the coastal scrub community, we include it here even though its flowers are tiny. They are for flower lovers with hand lenses. Eriogonum has pretty apple-blossom pink and white petals with six pink stamens and three styles. Wild buckwheat grows in compound inflorescences, which are very round and button-like. Blooming heavily in spring, some flowers may be found in just about any month of the year. All this on woody-based shrubs two or three feet high, often with some almost prostrate branches, thinly woolly, especially on the underside of their leaves. This buckwheat is common on dunes and flats behind the dunes and bluffs along the coast from Monterey County to San Diego County.

Wild buckwheat and its inland relatives are important bee plants. The early day "homegrown sage honey" was probably close to half buckwheat, strong, dark and yummy! I find it gentle fun to sit in the sand near buckwheat bushes and bee-watch. Even though they seem all business, getting several sips from one button makes it look like sort of a bee picnic!

5. CHAPARRAL

CHAPARRAL ADAPTATIONS

Many plants of this community have very interesting and diverse adaptations to soil, climate and fire in general. In the first place, the word chaparral is not the name of one plant; it describes a whole group (13 or more) of plants that grow in poor soil on steep, hot hillsides where it rarely rains from late spring until early winter. Think about that—eight or nine months without rain. Most of these woody evergreen shrubs have a wide network of roots; there is as much vegetative matter below ground as there is above, to soak up any and all moisture. There is usually no trunk, rather many branches, fifteen or more from a woody crown right at ground level. Many chaparral bushes have adventitious organs in the crown that can sprout new growth in just weeks after a fire has destroyed all above ground vegetation. Leaves are small or thick and leathery or felty-hairy, which helps to reduce water loss through normal transpiration. They can tolerate extremely hot and fairly cold temperatures. The evergreen foliage, especially new growth, is often heavily browsed. Many also have protective spines (modified twigs) to prevent over-consumption. Chaparral is mule deer country, as well as the haunt of wood rat, bobcat, brush rabbits, quail and mountain lion.

YUCCA—*Yucca whipplei* ssp. *percursa*

My first recollection of yuccas, also called Our Lord's Candle, was seeing them gleaming in scattered clumps along a winding mountain road. The bus chugged ever upward, well after dark, but we could still see the stately white flower candles all the way. I was going to summer camp, and ever since I've remembered yuccas as June bloomers often when the moon is full.

The sword-shaped leaves have a sharp spine on the tip and grow in a large rosette at ground level. The long tough fibers in the leaves were very useful to the Native Americans for cordage, belts, mats, nets, sunhats, etc. Leaves were pounded in water to release the fibers. Saponin (soap) was salvaged from the residual pulp and more saponin was extracted from yucca roots. This soap was used to wash hair during wedding rituals and baby-naming ceremonies by some groups. Ripe fruit was eaten raw or roasted and peeled (the outer skin is bitter). Young flowers were used in

soup after the green ovary was removed. The excellent book, *Maria: The Potter of Ildefonso* by Alice Marriott, describes how Maria's husband Julian applied the black-on-black design to their now-famous pottery with a yucca fiber brush.

The leaf rosette grows, storing energy in the crown for many years, then rapidly sends up a stout stalk five to 14 feet high on whose upper two or more feet develop the creamy white bell-shaped blossoms. The flowers hang downward, which seems convenient for their pollinators, a small white moth called tegeticula. This relationship between the moth and the candle must have evolved over a very long time, as the adult moth emerges from its pupa case in the soil, where it has spent the winter, at the time when the yucca flowers begin blooming. A female moth mates and then gathers sticky pollen from the anthers of a flower, packing it into a ball which she holds "under her chin." She then flies to another yucca plant in bloom. Here she puts her pollen ball on the stigma and actually pushes it into a cup-like depression on that fleshy organ. Dr. Meeuse says, "The shape of the front legs and the mouth parts and the way they operate are just right for this task." Then she crawls up in the pendulous flower to the ovary, where she oviposits her eggs. As the yucca seeds develop, the moth eggs hatch into tiny greenish larvae which feed on some of the growing seeds as the larvae molt and grow. The yucca pods are large with many divisions (in cross section rather like a grape-fruit), so many seeds mature to make yucca plants while others are food for the young of this moth that innately cross-pollinates these flowers. I love this interrelationship story which Meeuse describes as an "absolute masterpiece" in his chapter called "On the Wings of the Night" in his *Story of Pollination* book (see Further Reading List). Then there is the story of the little night lizard—zantusia, that lives in, on and because of the Joshua tree (another species: *Y. brevifolia*). I could go on and on, but will end with the pertinent observation of Dr. R.F. Hoover; "Yucca grassland is a unique local plant association near San Luis Obispo on hills where serpentine rock has not broken down completely into soil. *Yucca whipplei* is the dominant scenic feature." In our three central coast counties, the subspecies *percursa* is the common *Yucca whipplei* and it spreads by underground stems to form large colonies of genetically identical plants. In some other subspecies of *Yucca whipplei*, the entire plant dies following flowering. We must get out next spring and tap gently on the stalks of our yuccas to see if the little white moths fly out and back into the flowers, assuring us that genetic diversity is also being maintained by this wonderful interaction between the moth and the candle.

VETCH—*Vicia gigantea*
WILD SWEET PEA—*Lathyrus vestitus*
CHAPARRAL PEA—*Pickeringia montana*

In springtime, as we wander the lovely trails and backcountry roads of our three counties, these three members of the Pea Family—Leguminosae—will likely gladden the scene. They all have typical pea flowers with banners and keels and they all live mainly in the chaparral-covered hills so we are putting them together.

VETCH, naturalized from Europe, is a vine-like

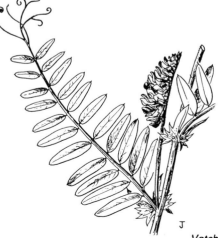

Vetch

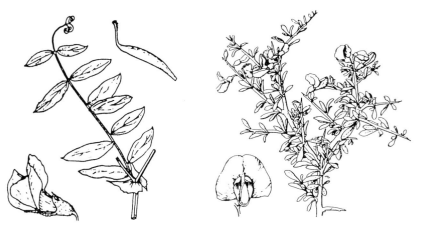

Wild Sweet Pea   Chaparral Pea

herb and a stout-stemmed perennial. It has many small leaflets on the tendril-bearing leaf stalk. The pretty flowers are reddish-purple fading to bluish. They are about one-half inch long, numerous and all usually crowded on one side of the stem. Vetch blooms in moist places March to June, near but not right on the coast.

WILD SWEET PEA is much like vetch, but more variable. Stems are angled and may grow low or climb by tendrils up to three feet if there is something to support them. Leaflets are six to 12, gray-green and finely hairy. The flowers are numerous, a little larger than vetch and white to pinkish, blooming February to May.

CHAPARRAL PEA has handsome bright pink to purplish flowers on a spiny evergreen shrub with stiff branches. The leaves are alternate, simple or with three leaflets, and on green twigs. This shrub rarely fruits in our area, but often spreads by underground stems, especially after fire. Widely distributed in the Santa Lucia, La Panza and San Luis Ranges, the Santa Ynez, San Rafael and Sierra Madre Mountains and on Santa Cruz Island, so Dr. Hoover thought it must have seeded here in the past. I first found pickeringia in the wild while coming down to Santa Barbara out of the Santa Ynez Mountains in April. We had three bushes at Rancho Santa Ana Botanic Garden. It was and still is a pleasure to meet flowers in nature that I'd learned to love in the garden.

PEARLY EVERLASTING—*Anaphalis margaritacea*

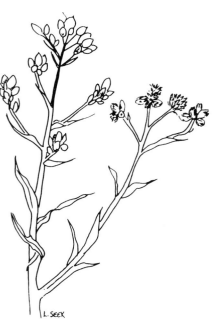

A white woody-based perennial with slender underground stems that form patches of erect stems which often become one to two feet tall. The narrow leaves, one to four inches long, are dark green and smooth on top and white and felty underneath. The many pearly bracts surrounding the flower head are the conspicuous feature of this plant.

The pearlies belong to the Everlasting Tribe of the Sunflower Family and they have evolved a life style quite different from many of their relatives; they have all staminate flowers on one plant, and all pistillate flowers on yet another plant. In other words the sexes are separated by plant rather than by arrangement on a flower head as in the other composites we've dealt with thus far. Botanists call this dioecious. Now we are challenged not only by a new word, but to find out which kind of flowers the pearly before us has! The first several plants I scrutinized with my hand lens had a tiny "nest" of bright yellow anthers down in the middle of the pearly bracts. These must be staminate plants, right? Recently I found a plant with several tiny yellow pistils rising a little above the pearly bracts. Now that we think we know what to look for, I'm eager to find these in different stages of maturity on their separate plants and perhaps become able to perceive how cross pollination occurs. So you see, now, what ongoing discoveries are possible for us happy flower lovers.

Pearly everlastings range the coastal regions from central California north. They have a vegetative kind of fragrance and I often see butterflies on them. We find them in the vegetated areas on the Morro Bay sand spit, in canyon bottoms and on north slopes along trails in the scrub as well as the chaparral.

FREMONTIA or FLANNEL BUSH—
Fremontodendron californicum

This "most spectacular" of native shrubs is much-branched, from four feet to small trees of 25 feet tall (with 30 foot spread) and trunk diameters up to 16 inches. Fremontia's mucilaginous inner bark was called slippery elm in the past. The leaves are alternate and variable in size and shape, though many are three-lobed, thick and leathery, dark green and downy-hairy like felt. The hairs may cause skin irritation to some people.

The flowers are large, yellow to orange-yellow, with no petals, but the showy calyx resembles a typical corolla. It is five-lobed, hairy outside, and usually smooth inside with five nectar-bearing pits at their base. (Young visitors at Rancho Santa Ana Botanic Garden liked to gently rub their little fingers in the nectaries of the cloned hybrid Fremontia California Glory, then lick and repeat until dragged onward along the path, with "Let's leave some nectar for the pollinators!") Fremontias have five stamens with large light yellow anthers; the numerous fruits, usually five-valved capsules, are bristly-hairy. The seeds inside are brown and smooth when ripe and need to be soaked in warm water overnight to germinate.

Botanists must struggle with the taxonomy of these variable shrubs but we flower lovers can settle for these three species: *F. mexicanum, F. californicum* and *F. decumbens,* and some truly lovely hybrids of which California Glory is my favorite. Other controlled hybrid clones worth looking into are F. Pacific Sunset, F. San Gabriel and F. Ken Taylor. F. California Glory has shallow-cupped, lemon-yellow flowers, all tending to open about the same time, which are produced in great abundance and spread along the branches for a long flowering period. F. Pacific Sunset has deep orange-yellow flowers—large (3 1/2 to 4 inch) saucer-shaped blossoms. F. San Gabriel has buttercup yellow flowers which are bell shaped and three inches across. Because of the nature of their branching, both of these espalier very well. F. Pacific Sunset has a longer blooming time than F. San Gabriel. F. Ken Taylor is a recently introduced hybrid that appears to have the low spreading growth habit of one of its three progenitors, *F. decumbens*, from Pine Hill, El Dorado County.

These beautiful plants have been both the joy and despair of gardeners ever since they were first cultivated. Unless their demanding cultural requirements can be met, you may be disappointed. They must have no water during the summer and should be planted where there is good natural drainage. Under favorable conditions fremontias, especially the hybrids, grow rapidly and may bloom the first season after planting in the fall.

My personal love affair with flannel bush goes back to school days, when a border of them grew between the Pacific Electric (the big red cars!) station and Pomona College in Claremont in southern California. They were large, free-growing and a riot of golden yellow blossoms beginning, I think, in March. Years later when I returned to Claremont to start the Youth Education Program at the botanic garden, Dr. Munz and I were reminiscing about the "good old days" and I mentioned that border. He was pleased that I had noticed and remembered because he had planted them himself when he taught at Pomona College, long before the botanic garden moved to Claremont.

We have F. California Glory bushes growing in the Morro Bay Library landscaping. They seem to manage to have a few large flowers most anytime I go by. I haven't thought I had room for one in my small native garden, but after writing this, I want at least one now more than ever!

COFFEEBERRY—*Rhamnus californica*

These evergreen shrubs with their lustrous black fruit, which is probably responsible for the common name, have oblong leaves one to three inches long with rather conspicuous veins. They are dark green above and paler underneath with mostly smooth edges. The tiny greenish white flowers are very numer-

ous, but it's easy to overlook them until they develop handsome berries in late autumn. They go through a long ripening period during which several color changes take place, first green, then yellow, dull red and finally black. We have several coffeeberry bushes at the Morro Bay Library where you can see all four colors on the same bush, making them especially attractive. If black ones almost fall off in your hand, taste a <u>few</u> (they are related to cascara, a well known laxative!). Usually there are two flattened-to-each-other dark seeds inside. One bumper crop year here in San Luis Obispo County our hiking group collected quite a few ripe berries and Allen Hanson made some jam. It was a lovely dark purple and tasted wildly good on crackers. Al saved the seeds for me. I soaked, strung and dried them. Winter evenings in front of the TV, I restrung them with other wild fruits, such as acorns, wild cucumber seeds, a few colored beads and dried kelp sections, making necklaces just for the fun of it or perhaps trying to identify with our long ago predecessors in their basic manipulation of things available in nature for decorative uses as well as food.

Coffeeberries grow readily from fresh seed. Young plants in gallon cans may be set out when a year or more old. They require sun, coarse soil and very little water.

HOLLYLEAF CHERRY or ISLAY—*Prunus ilicifolia*

This attractive evergreen shrub is scattered throughout the chaparral-covered hills and occasionally in the coastal scrub of our area. Its shining stiff leaves have wavy spine-tipped margins. The small white "roses" grow in dense and fairly long panicles, often abuzz with bees. The fruits (closely related to domestic cherries, plums, peaches and almonds) when ripe are red, more of less one-half inch in diameter with a thin sweetish pulp and a very large pit. Native Americans, perhaps more nutritionally aware than we, generally ignored their pulp, but used the large kernel inside the pit. After cracking, drying and grinding the seeds, the meal was leached in water through sand and boiled for soup.

Many animals eat hollyleaf cherry's fruit and buds—scrub and Steller's jays, raccoons and wood rats, among others. Mule deer browse the twigs, bark and foliage. Along the hiking trails in the San Gabriel Mountains above Claremont, I often found scat with six or eight hollyleaf cherry pits plainly visible in them. These droppings usually ended with a pointed tip of digestively-processed fur. I never learned for sure what animal ate these large fruits or what good was accomplished by doing so, but I suspected coyote. ¿Quien sabe?

Hollyleaf cherry is extensively planted as an ornamental. The Morro Bay Library has a specimen Catalina cherry (a near relative) in its patio center. The patio is also hedged around the two outsides with islay. Foliage sprays (prunings) with their glossy green leaves last several weeks and may be substituted for English holly with toyon berries for Christmas decorations.

BUSH POPPY—*Dendromecon rigida*

These lemon-yellow flowers have four rounded open petals and many stamens and grow on a medium sized shrub with smooth linear gray-green leaves that are evergreen. They are found on the hot south-facing slopes of steep chaparral and coastal scrub-covered hills. The long curved seed pods, packed full of tiny seeds, show this woody shrub's relationship to our herbaceous California poppy, but bush poppy pods split open from the bottom. Many seeds are eaten by birds and other wildlife and some grow into new plants. In late winter through spring, bush poppies put on quite a show on our hills. Along the Forest Service truck trail on east Cuesta Ridge, I found both vigorous seedlings and crown-sprouting bushes, just two years after a Las Pilitas fire. Marjorie Schmidt suggests burning pine needles or straw to germinate seeds, which surely hints to this plant's long journey through time with fire.

I first found these handsome shrubs in the wild in the Santa

Lucia Mountains in the late 1960s, though we had fine displays at Rancho Santa Ana Botanic Garden. There they are grown from cuttings of *D. harfordii*, a Channel Island species which has broader leaves and makes a nice garden plant. I have one in my yard that I got at the Yerba Buena Nursery in Woodside. It is doing well even though I keep "pruning" the flowers for bouquets. It has had some blossoms on the bush nearly all year around. (This plant is often called "tree poppy," but we prefer "bush" as it is not a single-trunk tree!)

CLIMBING PENSTEMON or
RED HONEYSUCKLE—*Keckiella cordifolia*

This plant with tubular red flowers can be found from mid-spring well into summer on north or east slopes of chaparral and coastal scrub-covered hills. It is a woody vining shrub that grows up through other bushes to flower above them and it also hangs out over trails where it attracts hummingbirds and flower lovers.

Keckiella was previously named penstemon. In the 1960s, taxonomists re-examined the genus penstemon and showed that some of the species could be separated from the rest on the basis of very woody stems, presence of a nectary ring around the base of the ovary, and lack of glandular hairs on the inside of the corolla tube. Thus seven penstemons with these characteristics were re-named keckia, but not for long, as it was then found that the name keckia had already been used for a genus of fossil algae. Never is the same scientific genus name given to two even quite different plants. When this is discovered, the last one must be changed. So keckia became keckiella, thus complying with the International Rules of Botanical Nomenclature. So our lovely climbing penstemon is officially keckiella—its species name remained the same.

After abundant rain in March of 1991 these handsome vine-like shrubs were blooming in profusion along the Forest Service back road to Lopez Lake from Pozo and in other parts of our area.

(Paraphrased with permission of the author, Dr. Dirk Walters, from an article in the September, 1988, California Native Plant Society newsletter.)

MANZANITA—*Arctostaphylos* spp.

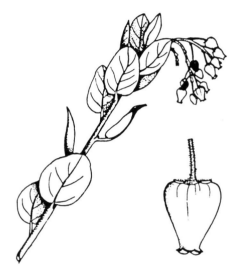

The common name is from the Spanish for "little apple," arcto-staph-(i)-los is from two Greek words meaning "bear berry" and it is a member of the Heather Family.

Manzanita is one of the most important shrubs in the chaparral community with more than 40 species in California and lots in our three counties; we chose to consider mainly the genus here. All have pretty urn-shaped white flowers often tinged with pink, that bloom in the winter and spring and have smooth reddish bark that is sloughed off in thin strips or curls as the plant grows; most have thick leathery evergreen leaves, usually held vertically. Several but not all manzanitas have a large woody root crown right at ground level. This structure, sometimes called a burl, sends out new shoots after the bush has been destroyed in a brush fire, a common and often natural event in areas where the crown sprouters are found. Utilizing the intact deep penetrating root system, it sprouts and grows a new top and will generally have an advantage over seedlings starting from "scratch." These manzanitas will make the same sprouting response to bulldozers, floods or severe pruning. However, the majority of manzanitas do depend on seed for reproduction, which they produce in copious quantities. Many grow and some become food for the wildlife with which they share this dynamic ecosystem. Those that grow in less fire prone areas make shallow, wide-spreading root systems, which do not anchor to underlying substrate, but do very well, often forming the climax community over large areas for long periods of time. Examples of two of these arctostaphylos species which have adopted different but vital life styles are Eastwood manzanita—*A. glandulosa,* a crown sprouter, and bigberry manzanita—*A. glauca,* a tree-like shrub which makes many seeds in large and relatively juicy "little apples."

Many species and clones of these beautiful shrubs with the angular red-brown trunks and branches, stiff green leaves and plentiful clusters of pinkish white flowers and roly-poly fruits are available in the horticultural trade. The clones are selections from species, the majority of which are hybrids or suspected hybrids. If you'd like to have some manzanitas growing in your own landscape, I earnestly suggest that you read the section on arctostaphylos (13 pages) in *California Native Trees and Shrubs* by Lenz and Dourley (see Further Reading List). This information is based on over 60 years of experience and careful records. Often there is confusion as to the true identity of nursery names and stock. This book includes a full page of leaf silhouettes to help in finding similar introductions to those described. Don't named clones like Sandsprite, Winterglow and Emerald Carpet sound tempting? If you select for your site and climate and follow their recommendations, especially as to water, you'll be rewarded with beautiful shrubs that need minimum work and water once you understand and meet their basic requirements.

PITCHER SAGE—*Lepechinia calycina*

This is a woody-based shrub with large loose clusters of rather pendulous pale lavender flowers. It grows on steep hillsides in dense chaparral. After the flowers have finished, the large dark seeds develop in the top of the persistent calyx which dries to look somewhat like a Japanese lantern. A relative to our many aromatic salvias, lepechinia is also in the Mint Family.

TOYON or CALIFORNIA HOLLY or CHRISTMAS BERRY—*Heteromeles arbutifolia*

The movie capital, Hollywood, was named for this shrub. It probably was in full red-berried fruit when the town was laid out. They bloom in June, July and August but hardly anyone notices the millions of tiny white roses. It's the berry that reddens by Thanksgiving and on through the Christmas season that attracts people. By January the berries are ripe and the birds begin eating them, disseminating the seeds far and wide. Migrating cedar waxwings eat many toyon berries while resting over a few days. At Rancho Santa Ana Botanic Garden we had a large bush which came from San Clemente or Santa Catalina Island (*H. arbutifolia* variety *macrocarpa*). The berries were large but birds did not readily eat them, apparently preferring the mainland species. Percy C. Everett, long-time Superintendent of Rancho Santa Ana Botanic Garden, enjoyed recommending to visiting garden groups that they plant at least one of each; one for the birds and the Island variety for their own long time enjoyment.

Toyon, an important element in the chaparral community, is a shrub or small "tree" (usually six to ten feet, but 25 feet is not uncommon). They are widely distributed and may also be found in foothill woodland but not usually above 3500 feet. These evergreen California hollies have dark green elliptical leaves that are thick, sharply toothed and up to four inches long and one and a half inches wide. The flowers are numerous, small and white and in large terminal clusters. The fruits are large groups of bright red berry-like pomes (apples and toyon berries are structurally similar, both being members of the Rose Family).

Christmas berries have been in cultivation for at least 100 years. The glowing winter berries enliven many miles of freeway. Because of its deep root system it is useful for soil stabilization and erosion control. It is also recommended as an accent plant, a rough hedge and especially in a mixed border of drought-tolerant native shrubs. Toyon can be propagated from fresh seed. Plants should be held in cans the first year and planted out in the second autumn. Usually a dense shrub, it can be pruned in winter when the berries are cut for decoration.

Toyon berries were used as food and drink by Native Americans and early settlers. The flowers are a source of honey. Many birds relish its berries and in the dry winters of 1990-91 we saw evidence of deer browsing as high as they could reach in the Rinconada area.

PINK-FLOWERING or WINTER CURRANT—
Ribes sanguineum, var. *glutinosum*

This erect, spreading deciduous shrub grows four to six feet high, has three-lobed round green leaves, which often are wider than long and with lobes slightly toothed. The pendulous flower clusters are a deeper pink than any other wild ribes I've found. Winter currant occurs in open spaces among brush and trees in chaparral, foothill woodland and mixed evergreen forest at elevations below 2000 feet. I have found these rosy-pink lovelies in bloom along the Cerro Alto trail in early December. The flowers are followed, after pollination, by dark glandular berries. Horticulturists think that this is the most beautiful of the native currants. Ribes have been in cultivation for many years (there are 31 species of ribes in California and it was hard to narrow down to just three "jewels" in our three-county part of the state). Pink-flowering currant is moderately drought tolerant; it does better in gardens with some careful watering.

FUCHSIA-FLOWERING GOOSEBERRY—
Ribes speciosum

Certainly one of our most spectacular native shrubs in bloom, it is tall, deciduous, has numerous horizontal branches and sharp and plentiful spines. The leaves are round with three shallow lobes, leathery texture, deep green above and paler beneath. The deep crimson flowers hang down from the branches. The stamens hang way below the small petals. The fair-sized fruit is a bristly berry, edible if you can beat the wildlife to them. Split <u>one</u> open and turn it inside-out into your mouth; worth a few finger pricks for the wild, sour, semi-sweet taste! Leave the rest for the permanent residents. Fuchsia-flowered gooseberry bloomed heavily at RSABG in Claremont when the migrating hummingbirds came through in spring. I loved to sit on a bench nearby at noon and watch the bronze beauties challenge the larger resident Annas hummingbirds for "their" bushes!

Widespread in the central coast, *R. speciosum* blooms as early as January and on into May, usually on north-facing slopes.

CHAPARRAL or CANYON CURRANT—*Ribes malvaceum*

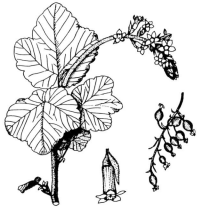

This erect deciduous shrub grows to eight feet tall and has stout stems with brown bark and rough leaves which are three to five-lobed, toothed, glandular and aromatic. The half-inch flowers hang in drooping clusters of 25 or more blossoms, light pink to bright rose, occasionally nearly white. Its berries are small, blue to black, sometimes with a whitish bloom, or somewhat glandular and hairy. This wild currant can be found in all three counties below 2500 feet in elevation. They bloom from February through April.

Note: All the currants and gooseberries are in the genus ribes; the gooseberries have spines and prickles, the currants do not.

INDIAN WARRIOR—*Pedicularis densiflora*

The green leaves are finely cut with tiny teeth on the edges and form an attractive basal rosette below the eight to 20-inch tall spikes of pretty purple-red flowers. They usually seem to be mixed in with many reddish bracts, but careful viewing reveals the two-lipped corolla with the lower lip short and the upper lip wider, longer and arched a bit with a tiny bent-down tip. Usually some of the four stamens show. The genus name is from "louse," due to an old superstition that sheep eating it became lousy. Indian warrior blooms in January through April on dry slopes in the chaparral and near streams in mixed woods.

I first saw these dark red lovelies in the Santa Lucia Mountains on a week-long camping-hiking trip while I still lived in southern California and thought them vaguely reminiscent of old familiars from trips in the High Sierra. They are in the same genus with elephant heads and the same Figwort Family with monkey flowers and paint brushes and, like them, are a partial parasite on the roots of neighboring woody plants.

These warm red flowers were the first conspicuous blooms at the west end of the burned area after the August 1994 Highway 41 fire. They appeared to benefit from the extra light, nutrients in the ashes and gentle continuous rains following the removal of their usual shrub canopy. Elsewhere in the Santa Lucia Mountains I've seen Indian warriors also growing well in disturbed areas.

WOOLLY BLUE CURLS—*Trichostema lanatum*

With its extravagant profile, woolly blue curls runs the color gamut from blue to rose-violet in its furry buds. Another member of the Mint Family, trichostema is a woody shrub in the steep chaparral-clad hills. It gets hikers' attention when it blooms in early spring. It's fun to watch a bee, which has sipped nectar, back out of this fairly deep-throated flower and along the four lengthy slender stamens,

sometimes somersaulting into flight as the anthers dust it with pollen.

COAST TASSEL BUSH—*Garrya elliptica*

The unusual flowers of this shrub will surely get your attention when you find one in bloom in the hills in mid winter. A really spectacular display was put on by one along the north fork of Islay Creek in Montaña de Oro State Park one recent dry winter. The tassels or catkins were over a foot long and the large bush was loaded with them. Garryas have male catkins on one bush and female catkins on a different bush and the pollen is wind-transferred. The male flowers are gray-green or yellow-green, the catkins being a series of tiny upside-down cups with the stamens hanging out

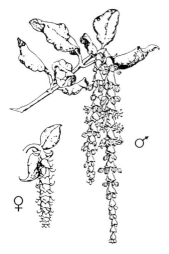

below the rims. The female flower's catkins are short, stout and have whiskery stigmas peeking out of sheaths, where the berries develop after fertilization. Tassel bush has crisp undulate leaves that are evergreen and leathery. They are shiny above and felted with woolly hairs below.

Garrya veatchii is perhaps commoner in San Luis Obispo County (smaller shrub with smaller catkins). We chose *G. elliptica* because it occurs in all three counties and has more horticultural value, especially the male plants with their tassels standing out against the thick dark green foliage. They prefer full sun, tolerate dryness, and the tassels will look better longer if protected from the wind. In nature, coast tassel bush is found on dry slopes and ridges below 2000 feet in the evergreen forest and chaparral communities.

CLEMATIS or VIRGIN'S BOWER—*Clematis lasiantha*

These names bring at once to my mind's eye visions of garlands of creamy white blossoms or seed plumes draped gracefully and abundantly over the chaparral shrubs along the Cerro Alto trail in the Los Padres National Forest off State Highway 41 between Atascadero and Morro Bay. Clematis can be found throughout our three counties and blooms as early as February and is still much in evidence with its handsome seed pom-poms until the late spring winds carry the long curved plumes and small seeds off and away to places where a new vine can grow.

Clematis is a woody climber, the attractive compound leaves have three leaflets and the inch-wide flowers grow up out of the leaf and stem axil on rather long stems.

Note for interior decorators and dried flower arrangement buffs: My sister-in-law carefully clipped off about three feet of clematis vine loaded with fluffy pom-poms, laid it over newspapers in the luggage compartment of her car and sprayed it very carefully with hair spray. She closed the back end and went home. Her Thanksgiving table with the usual colorful gourds, pumpkins, etc. overlaid by her clematis seed garland was lovely.

PRICKLY PHLOX—*Leptodactylon californicum*

Its flowers are funnelform, rose, lavender-pink or white and in terminal clusters. The stamens grow in the corolla tube at <u>one</u> level, whereas in the phlox genus they grow at different levels. These truly pretty flowers grow on a low semi-woody perennial shrub with very prickly needle-like light green leaves thick on the stems. Widespread in wet years on dry slopes in foothill woodland and coastal scrub as well as chaparral, prickly phlox blooms from March into June. San Luis Obispo County may be its northern limit.

For gardens it can be grown from seed, and once plants are established, seedlings will start up voluntarily. They require sun and semi-dry locations. Useful on terraces or among boulders, young plants flower abundantly and make very colorful displays, and will bloom on and off through the year. After about five years, prickly phlox gets straggly and should be replaced with young plants.

MATILIJA POPPY—*Romneya coulteri*

This large white flower (to nine inches across) with the conspicuous yellow center (anthers surrounding a knobby green stigma) is one of the glamour girls among native plants. The petals unpack themselves from the tight bud like ballerina skirts coming out of a trunk, still a little pleated and crinkled. The genus which was discovered by Thomas Coulter has only two species: *R. coulteri*

and *R. trichocalyx*. The flower used to grow profusely in Matilija Canyon in Ventura County, hence the common name, which may be of Chumash origin.

Once common from Santa Barbara County into northern Baja California, it is now mostly found in cultivation. Specimen bushes or hedges flower from June to September and need no extra water once established, but may become quite invasive, as romneya is a perennial with creeping underground root stocks. Huge flowered hybrids between the two species are available from most nurseries and worth a try.

INTRODUCTION TO THE CALIFORNIA LILACS—*Ceanothus* spp.

California lilac indeed! No <u>real</u> lilac this, thought I, having moved rather reluctantly from the midwest to California at a tender age. Time softens many things, even attitudes. So when grown, married and playing pioneers on 19 acres of brush south of Lake Elsinore, California lilac and I became fast friends. My spouse and I liked to hike up the fire road in the spring in the Santa Ana Mountains across the narrow valley from our home. Thus we got acquainted with the chaparral in bloom. We tried growing ceanothus from seed and learned much by trial and error that is now available in many publications. But it was fun and one of our first big successes was with a deep blue ceanothus from across the way. The capsules of our chosen shrub, when mature and dry enough, popped open explosively, firing the seed every which way. So we tied several small cheese cloth sacks around heavy-fruited branch ends and in due time caught quite a few of the small seeds. We planted them in various ways and the "leftovers" I took down to the bottom of our veggie garden, scratched up a three foot by four foot area, scattered the seed on it and prayed and danced for rain and it did! Fourteen little seedlings grew, had to be thinned (so very hard for me to do). When they first bloomed, we celebrated. They were not all deep blue like their parent 'tis true, but they were beautiful and they were "ours." Thus I became a staunch defender of the California lilac, especially if anyone from the midwest compared them to "theirs" which are of Persian origin.

Now we get down to business with a rather direct "translation" from Munz' *A California Flora* and its general introduction to the genus ceanothus: shrubs or small trees with spreading branches, sometimes spiny twigs, sometimes with dark corky bumps. Leaves mostly persistent, frequently toothed, some three-veined from the base, some with one main vein with laterals. Flowers small but showy, white, blue, purplish and sometimes lavender or pinkish, in terminal or lateral clusters. Sepals five, petal-like. Petals five, distinct, hooded and clawed. Stamens five, usually with short filaments. Ovary three-lobed, with a short three cleft style. Fruit a three-lobed capsule separating (some explosively) in maturity. Seed smooth, convex on one side. Between 50 and 60 species in temperate North America, many of horticultural value, hybridizing freely.

(Greek, *keanothus*, name used by Dioscorides for some spiny plant.)

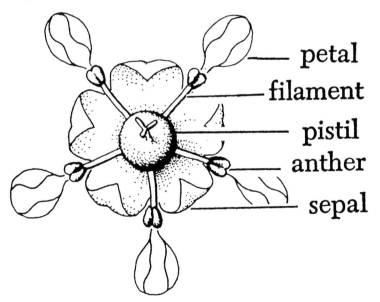

petal
filament
pistil
anther
sepal

Pictured is a typical ceanothus flower. Note the hooded aspect of the petals mentioned in the paragraph above. The petals being clawed means, in this case, that they extend out from the center. In our drawing, the extending claw portions of the petals are hidden from view by the filaments.

BUCKBRUSH—*Ceanothus cuneatus*

A most widely distributed California lilac, buckbush is an important component of the chaparral community though not confined to it. Growing up to 6000 feet in elevation, it can also be found in yellow pine forests. Buckbrush hybridizes with other species where it comes in contact with them. An erect shrub to eight feet, with diverging branches and short, stout, unequal branchlets. Buckbrush leaves are small, gray-green with one mid vein and usually a slight notch at the top and dark corky bumps on the twigs at the base of the leaves. The tiny flowers are white, rarely lavender and are densely clustered together. The round fruits have tiny horns atop each of the three sections of the seed capsule.

Formerly very prevalent in the Los Osos area of San Luis Obispo County. A few truly perceptive and well-informed people have kept them in their yards along with the scrub oaks. After choosing other natives for interplanting, they have their own mini-elfin forest of unique and primeval beauty as well as total drought and frost tolerance.

DEERBRUSH—*Ceanothus integerrimus*

This handsome loosely-branched shrub (to twelve feet tall) has greenish bark on the branches and flexible twigs and is never spiny. Found from 400 to 1500 feet in elevation in the Santa Lucias, deerbrush is often grouped with the montane or yellow pine chaparral community also.

This California lilac's flowers are in long feathery plumes of tiny, dense compound clusters which are six inches long and four inches wide. Deerbrush varies in color from white, pale to deep blue and pinkish to rose-lavender, (you see, we really can't tell which lilac we are looking at by color alone!), deerbrush blossoms beautifully in April to early August. The leaves are light green and smooth with three distinct main veins from the base and are semi-deciduous. Its fruits are round to triangular capsules, small, sticky and slightly depressed on top.

CHAPARRAL WHITETHORN—*Ceanothus leucodermis*

This California lilac is a stout shrub which grows to twelve feet tall with rigid, widely-divergent, spiny branches, which are gray or white in color. The leaves are an inch and a half long and a half inch wide, three-veined from the base, hairless but covered with a waxy powder both on top and underneath. Whitethorn's flower clusters are simple, short and dense, but occasionally are three inches long; they vary in color from white to a lovely pale blue to quite blue and may be found in bloom from April to June. The fruits are rounded, small and sticky.

I have long had trouble coping with the numerous species of California lilacs and their variability, but this is one I remember well from hiking foothill trails in southern California, so I was glad to find it here in all three counties of the central coast in chaparral and foothill woodland communities as well. Its gray-white bark, powdery leaves and light blue flowers give whitethorn an ethereal quality that contrasts rather sharply with its darker neighbors. I have a healthy respect for its thorns, which are modified twig ends. They are true thorns, not spines which are usually modified leaves. Next after poison oak, they are number two reason for staying on the trails!

HAIRY CEANOTHUS—*Ceanothus oliganthus*

This California lilac is a medium-sized shrub to ten feet tall, with numerous short, stiff branches that are densely shaggy with long soft hairs and a reddish warty bark. Branch ends sometimes become spiny when the leaves drop off. The leaves can be one and one half inches long and one inch wide. They are three-veined from the base, the top surface dark green with scattered longish hairs, the underside is paler green with scattered hairs especially on the veins. Hairy ceanothus flowers are loose, simple clusters to two inches long with colors ranging from deep blue or purple to almost white and blooming from late January to June. These attractive "whiskery" bushes are found on dry slopes below 4500 feet not much north of San Luis Obispo County.

BLUE BLOSSOM—*Ceanothus thyrsiflorus*

This California lilac is a large shrub, sometimes tree-like to 25 feet tall, with angled green flexible branches that don't become thorny. The bark on the trunk is thin and brownish. Blue blossom's leaves are two inches long and three quarters of an inch wide, three-veined from the base, dark green and smooth on top, with a few coarse hairs on the prominent veins underneath. The flower clusters are compound, to three inches long, light to deep blue to almost white and sometimes fragrant. (I suspect the air temperature and time of day have a bearing on whether we get the pleasing whiffs or not.) Fruits are slightly lobed, glandular, sticky and black when ripe. Blue blossom is found on wooded slopes and in canyons of the ocean side of the coast ranges of our area, usually below 2000 feet in chaparral and redwood/broadleaf evergreen communities where they bloom from February to June. In Monterey County, the variety *C.t. repens*—creeping blue blossom, is also found. This prostrate shrub has landscape potential for rock gardens.

GREENBARK LILAC or REDHEART— *Ceanothus spinosus*

This large shrub or small tree grows to 20 feet tall with a large root crown and is quite long lived. It has an open crown of upright branches with smooth greenish bark and spiny twigs on its horizontal branches. Redheart lilac's leaves are thick, leathery, smooth and shiny on both sides, one-veined from the base, one inch long and a half inch wide with smooth margins. The compound flower clusters grow to six inches long and are pale blue to nearly white, and fragrant. They bloom February to May. The small fruits are divided into three sections, sticky but becoming smoother and dark when mature.

Greenbark ceanothus may be found on dry slopes in coastal mountains below 3000 feet where it is a member of coastal scrub and chaparral communities.

6. OAK GRASSLAND

SHELL CREEK'S PERSIAN CARPET

When I think of the oak grassland community, immediately my mind's eye sees Shell Creek. A special place in special springs is this area in eastern San Luis Obispo County. The name comes from an intermittent stream that rises in the nearby La Panza Range. Shell Creek Road begins at Highway 58 just west of the culvert over the stream bed, and goes north to Shandon. A sandstone ledge is north and vaguely parallel with Highway 58; along it grow live oaks and gray pines. In the good sized pasture here, when the rains are right, lies one of the most lovely living "Persian carpets" I've ever seen. I made pilgrimages out there for nine years until April of 1988 when I finally viewed this living miracle. I hope you too may experience it some year. Let's slip back to that April when the photo on page C-4 was taken (standing a foot higher than usual on a thoughtfully offered step stool). As my camera and I reveled over the colorful field, it came to me that probably I'd died and gone to Heaven, it was so beautiful! But the flowers were alive, growing, being visited by pollinators and making seed to lie waiting on the ground for optimum conditions to come again.

On the way east from Santa Margarita on Highway 58 you pass cliffs festooned with pink prickly phlox and blue "lakes" of lupine growing under the blue oaks just beginning to leaf out. Where the Shell Creek Road and the stream cut through the rocky ledge, the charming thistle sage with its fringed lavender petals and red anthers is found.

The county has installed metal barriers along Shell Creek Road to help us remember to leave only footprints and take only pictures.

Below is a list of flowers typically found at Shell Creek in early April. I've probably overlooked several, so we've left room for you to add your future discoveries.

Golden-yellows: California poppy, fiddleneck, California dandelion, tidy tips, violets, gold fields and various coreopsis species.

Blues: lupine (several species), baby blue eyes, phacelia, violets, thistle sage and blue dicks.

Red-violets: owl's clover, Chinese houses, clarkias and scarlet bugler.

Whites: popcorn flower, cream cups and low large evening primroses in the creek bed.

COAST LIVE OAK—*Quercus agrifolia*

This is our commonest native evergreen tree near, but not on, the coast. It grows in canyons, on north-facing slopes, on stabilized sandy plains and scattered eastward through our area. Wait a minute—an oak tree in a wildflower book? Oaks don't have blossoms! Sure they do—how else acorns?

Acorn meal, mush cakes and water biscuits were the staff of life to the coastal Native Californians who lived here for thousands of years before we came. To them, *Q. agrifolia* acorns were prized. Acorns of other species of oaks were gathered chiefly as an emergency food.

In early spring, oak trees have a golden glow. Step up close to see many, many tiny

yellow catkins. Brush a finger through to feel the fine yellow pollen. The tiny female flowers are harder to find. They are tucked among new leaves near the tips of twigs. They'll mature later on this tree to avoid self-pollination. Acorns develop under the miniscule stigmas after fertilization, and ripen in late fall.

VALLEY or WHITE OAK—*Quercus lobata*

Many people think that all California oaks are evergreen, but this is one of our most attractive **deciduous** oaks. They are found in warm inner coastal valleys in rich loamy soils, often in open park-like stands. A drive from Jolon through the Hunter-Liggett Military Reserve to the Nacimiento River is a good way to experience these large graceful trees whose scattered groves occupied much of the great central valley of California when there were fewer of us and more of them. Valley oak's huge erect trunks are grayish white with deeply furrowed bark. The trunk leads 50 to 120 feet up to the large rounded crown,

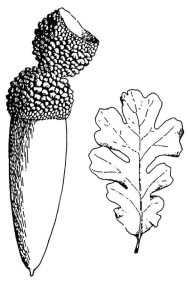

which in mature trees has drooping branches as well. White oak's leaves are three to five-lobed, often broader toward the end, but quite variable in size and form even on the same tree; green above, paler underneath and turning brown when shed in autumn. Valley oak's flowers are small yellow-green catkins and wee bashful ovaries feathered with minute stigmas, often a brownish maroon color. Wind pollinated plants like these have their numerous catkins out in spring breezes before the new leaves appear. Watch for a yellow haze in the bare crowns next spring.

According to A.L. Kroeber, "Galls which grow on valley oaks were collected by Native Californians for their juice, which was diluted and used as an eye wash." Of the deciduous oaks, valley oak was first choice for "acorn soup or mush, the chief daily food for more than three-fourths of interior Native California."

MEXICAN ELDERBERRY—*Sambucus mexicana*

The generic name is from the Greek for sambuke, a musical instrument made of elderwood. A deciduous shrub or small tree, well located individuals reach 30 feet and spread gracefully. A rapid grower, elderberry's new branches are pithy and break easily until hardened. Of the three commonest elderberries, *S. mexicana* is probably the one we are most apt to find, as it occurs on open flats, valleys and canyons from central California to northern Baja. In our area it is sparsely scattered in coastal scrub, chaparral and oak woodland, below 4500 feet in elevation. The other two are blue elderberry—*S. caerulea*—and red elderberry—*S. racemosa;* both are commoner farther north. The leaves of Mexican elderberry are pinnately compound with three to five leaflets, with the fifth one often larger. All leaflets have fine teeth along the margins but are smooth tipped. The numerous, tiny, creamy-white, pleasantly scented flowers are packed in flat-topped clusters, sometimes quite broad. They bloom from March through September followed by the spherical dark blue berries which have a whitish tinge. In dry years they grow only a little, make a few flowers and berries and drop their leaves in September and hang in there for better times—an admirable example of adaptation to our variable climate.

The literature is rife with tales about uses of this hardy little tree. The stems were used by people in several different countries to make arrow shafts, whistles and flutes (see Greek origin of genus name) and think on this evidence of convergent evolution by distant cultures over time! For me, the bottom line is that elderberries make a source of summer food for birds and other wildlife.

TREE TOBACCO—*Nicotiana glauca*

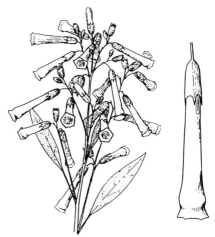

This large genus is found mostly in the American hemisphere and our most conspicuous tall shrub or small tree with the bright yellow tubular flowers comes to us from South America, perhaps as seeds in soil used for ballast in sailing ships. Found along dry stream beds and rocky banks, tree tobacco is widely scattered in both eastern and western parts of our area. The pendulous flowers are one to two inches long and spread open very slightly. The green calyx is tubular, short, five-cleft and persistent around the ovary which matures into a capsule containing many tiny seeds after fertilization. The leaves are light green, ovate, smooth-edged and on long stems.

Our local native tobaccos are mostly small white-flowered annuals, often glandular and viscid. These were used by Native

Americans for rituals and ceremonial purposes, not for "pleasure" smoking. In Santa Barbara County as early as 1875, plant collectors found *N. clevelandii* around shell mounds near Point Conception.

Tree tobacco is in the Nightshade Family along with tomatoes, eggplant and other edibles. Another nightshade, *N. tabacum*, an early domesticate, got its Latin name from an aboriginal American name from which also comes the word tobacco. In tropical America these tobacco plants were cultivated from earliest times and often "ran wild." Our genus was named for J. Nicot, French ambassador to Portugal who introduced tobacco into France about 1560. In the early 1970s, birders were observing that two species of hummingbirds that used to go further south were wintering over in California. The abundance of tree tobacco (which grows quickly in disturbed places) was given a good share of the credit, as it often has some flowers year around. Hummingbirds are fickle pollinators but one can't help but admire their adaptability! Though somewhat weedy, tree tobacco is fast growing, a very low water user and can be kept pruned and neat so we can enjoy the hummers they attract.

MILKWEED—*Asclepias* spp.

This soft woolly perennial with the milky sap can be found in dry gravelly stream beds, on rocky hillsides and in disturbed areas below 3000 feet, generally away from the coast. The interesting flowers are probably a delight to technical botanists as well as to flower lovers due to their unusual structures like hoods, horns, pollinia and winged anthers inside a tent-like pavilion. I have yet to find out how pollination is accomplished, though I suspect self-pollination occurs of which the illustrious C. Darwin said "nature seems to abhor." Anyone with light on this matter and willing to contact the publisher will be greatly appreciated by the author. The big furry umbels of flowers are easily recognized among or above the soft woolly leaves and who among us has not as a child taken the large opening pods and blown the hairy tufted seeds as high as possible, just to watch them drift gracefully away?

We here on the central coast are very aware of the importance of milkweed to Monarch butterfly caterpillars, because the adult Monarchs spend the winter with us in great numbers. Then with spring they move east and north, generation after generation, to find milkweed plants on which the females lay their eggs. Milkweeds were found to have many uses by the early people who lived here before Europeans arrived. Flowers were eaten raw or boiled and the buds were boiled for soup or with meat. Perhaps the most common use among all groups throughout California was as chewing gum. Milkweeds were frequently used as a medicinal herb, and in this connection it is interesting to note that milkweed was entered in the U.S. pharmacopoeia for treatment of various chest and lung ailments until 1936. The genus asclepias is named after Asklepios, the Greek god of medicine. Probably the most dependable use of milkweed was for its tough fibers, which could be made into rope, cord and coarse cloth. Fibers were taken from the stems, which were collected early in winter. Sometimes these were blended with Indian hemp, *Apocynum cannabinum*. Stems of milkweed probably were not soaked to release the fibers. The bark was removed and the fibers released by rubbing between the hands, then drawing the mass of fibers over a stock of smooth wood. The cord was rolled with skill and dexterity on the thigh much as was done with yucca, agave and some grasses.

JIMSON WEED—*Datura meteloides*

As you drive the back country roads of our area, you can still find this noxious perennial weed with the beautiful flowers in sandy or gravelly open spaces in scrub and grassland. A sprawling plant with big gray-green leaves, it's the corollas that get the attention of flower lovers and challenges photographers. Opening in the evening, the large erect trumpet-shaped blooms with five teeth are white shading to lavender as they fade in the morning after pollination. Note how the long flower buds are rolled up lengthwise, making a lovely pattern. Their prickly seed pods nod as they mature and open to drop light brown seeds.

The whole genus datura is **poisonous**. All parts of the plants, including seeds, have narcotic properties. Some species were used by Native Americans in tribal rites. Current revival of interest in and respect for the ancient cultures we overwhelmed with ours is commendable and shared by this writer. But, empirical attempts to emulate prehistoric uses of these plants have met with fatal results.

BLAZING STAR—*Mentzelia* spp.

My first recollection of this stunning yellow-orange flower on hairy, barbed plants is along a mountain trail rather late in autumn. There were just a few flowers with conspicuous and numerous gold-wire stamens with little packages of pollen atop them. They were on a dry stickery-leafed plant covered with interesting tubular seed pods with little dry pointed sepals around the open top. When I bent one slightly and tapped it over my open hand many small seeds slid out.

Blazing star belongs to a large genus of plants covered with barbed hairs. It has stiff much-divided leaves and satiny five-petaled flowers about one and one half to three inches across. In our section of California they are mostly in the warm dry interior areas, in dry stream beds, along roadsides and trails in sunny openings away from trees. Some species are annuals and come in wildflower seed packets, others are perennial. Some have orange at the base of the petals which may attract pollinators, others have pale yellow, long narrow petals. Some species like the one in the drawing grow on hills whose slopes are quite barren. In a year of good rainfall they are abundant and showy with vivid orange petals with a copper-red base.

Marjorie Schmidt chose *M. lindleyi* to describe in her *Growing California Native Plants* book. It was probably the one in my mixed seed packet. She advises to "broadcast seed in autumn on lean, well-drained soil. Blazing star can provide bright color and is especially valuable with plants having blue flowers. Several penstemons, phacelias or small lupines make suitable companions."

PRICKLY POPPY—*Argemone munita*

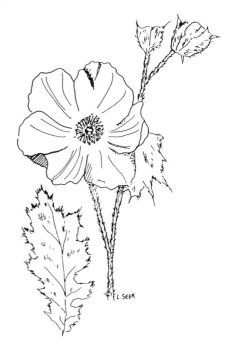

A robust often-branching herbaceous plant literally covered with stiff hairy spines and growing two to four feet high, it is occasional to frequent on flood plains of creeks, rivers and disturbed places, recent burns and along mountain roads in the eastern areas of all three counties. Prickly poppy has surprisingly green pinnate leaves underneath all those prickles. Out of this armed fortress emerge the lovely white flowers, three or four inches across and often gently crinkled on the first opening. Bright orange stamens surround the very short style topped by a knobby stigma. The oblong seed pods have three or more valves which open at the top and contain many black seeds.

Prickly poppy may be grown as a border for its showy six-petaled flowers. Collect branches with several pods when the first one opens and hang them upside down over newspapers in a warm dry place. You'll have seeds to share as well as to replant your cleared and cultivated border. In late fall, say November or after the first good rain, scatter the seeds and lightly press them in with the back of the rake. Thin the seedlings as needed. In nature, after a wet winter they bloom from March into July. In the garden with very little watering, only as needed, the blooming period can be extended if desired.

FIDDLENECK—*Amsinckia* spp.

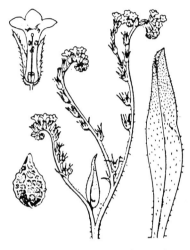

After wet winters, these rather weedy annuals make great swaths of yellow-orange all over the open spaces of the inner coast ranges and valleys. Other relatives (they have many) decorate sand dunes, marsh edges and headlands along the coast of Santa Barbara (plus the four Channel Islands), San Luis Obispo and Monterey Counties. Annuals in the Borage or Forget-me-not Family, fiddleneck lures us closer with its voluminous herbage and showy, bright-colored flowers. They have erect and spreading branches and stems that are rather acrid smelling, bristly and one to two feet tall. The leaves are alternate and the flowers rise out of scorpioid clusters that are also prickly-haired. The corolla varies from orange to yellow and is tubular, flaring out at the top. The stamens and threadlike style are down in the tube. The stigma is a two-lobed head. The ovary usually forms four one-seeded nutlets. Some day you may be sitting in a field of fiddlenecks with your hand lens and camera and realize you'd really like to know what species this one is. You will need to get well acquainted with its mature nutlets to find out. W. Amsink, an early nineteenth-century patron of the botanic garden in Hamburg, may have started this way, and he got a whole genus of orange-yellow flowers named after him!

PRINCE'S PLUME—*Stanleya pinnata*

This four-petaled member of the huge Mustard Family appears to have explored its way over to our area from the southwestern deserts by way of the Cuyama Valley and the flood plain of the Santa Maria River. It also grows on dry hills up to 5000 feet and is tolerant of soils containing gypsum.

Prince's plume has a woody base, grows to three or four feet high, and has much-divided leaves at the base and simple long narrow ones higher up, all are gray-green. The lovely light yellow flowers, each a half inch long with conspicuous stamens, grow on tall terminal spikes and bloom April to September. The seed pods are slender and one to three inches long.

Prince's plume takes up the mineral selenium from the soil. It uses it in place of sulfur in making amino acids, important building blocks of protein which we and all living organisms need to survive. Selenium can be toxic to mammals, including us, so this attractive plant is not popular with ranchers. Native Americans used the young leaves for greens. They boiled the leaves, then drained off the water and finished cooking them in fresh water. They knew it would make them sick if the first water was not thrown away. Our high-tech culture has made rapid strides in many ways, but also lost many wise old ways with the deculturization of the indigenous people. This plant was named for Edward Stanley, Earl of Darby 1773-1849, an ornithologist and once president of the Linnean Society.

DOUGLAS COREOPSIS—*Coreopsis douglasii*
BIGELOW COREOPSIS—*Coreopsis bigelovii*
LEAFY STEM COREOPSIS—*Coreopsis calliopsidea*

We are lumping three annual herbaceous relatives of giant coreopsis together here because these bright yellow daisy-like flowers will surely catch your eye when out hiking or driving in the spring months of March through to June. They are usually single flowers on long stems and put on fine displays after wet winters. All three are to be found in our three counties. We can "guesstimate" which one we are looking at by where we are on the map.

Douglas coreopsis is usually more widespread in the middle-eastern areas, on sandy or gravelly soils. It is less abundant in Santa Barbara County, but occasional about banks of

Douglas Coreopsis

woodland-chaparral where it blooms in April and on to June. The leaves are narrow, light green and basal. The large single flowers are bright yellow with solid centers. It has been found growing on serpentine right around the city of San Luis Obispo.

In years of good rainfall, bigelow coreopsis may be found further east on gravelly or sandy soils. This flower is frequent and colorful in disturbed places, on banks along trails and roads in chaparral-woodland. It blooms April through June.

Leafy stem coreopsis grows several stems from the base. Its foliage is divided and redivided into linear lobes and is light green. The flowers are single with wide golden rays forming a two-inches-across blossom. Found still further east in dry, open and gravelly places, it can make lovely swaths of deep yellow in wet years. This one usually blooms in March through May.

Coreopsis can be grown from seed in your garden. Plants will flower early if seeded in November or December. Open, sunny, somewhat sheltered areas with sandy loam are suggested. I had a few herbaceous coreopsis plants in my native garden the first few years. They were showy and thrifty, but the long flower stems tended to lie down before blooming and they died out. I suspect Morro Bay's salty winds were not to their liking. Take heed and choose natives suitable to your climate, soil, etc.

POPCORN FLOWER—*Plagiobothrys nothofulvus*

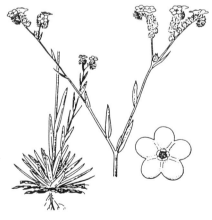

The pretty little hairy, uncurling coils of white flowers are commonly scattered across open grassy woodland pastures and pristine fields of coastal areas and inland to Cuyama Valley. They belong to the Borage Family and may bloom from February to June. The tubular corolla with five turned-out lobes is included in the calyx which is also hairy. The hairs are weak and slender, but prickly and often tawny or brown. The lower part of this plant has a purple dye.

Another member of the Borage Family which we flower-lovers can confuse with popcorn flower is *Cryptantha intermedia* which P. Munz suggested might be called white forget-me-not. To tell them apart, let's look at their characteristics. Popcorn flowers are generally larger, with softish tawny hairs on the coil and purple base; white forget-me-not has stiffer hairs, no purple dye and generally smaller flowers. The latter is commonly found in spring in open dry places and on burns in the chaparral, never near the sea, but inland to the western edge of the Carrizo Plain.

TIDY TIPS—*Layia platyglossa*

These handsome spring annuals have large yellow ray flowers that are usually tipped with creamy white, though sometimes they are all yellow. Tidy tips are common in all three counties on the coastal dunes, sea bluffs and inland valleys, where they, with other wildflowers, form the colorful carpets still to be found in some places. This member of the Tarweed Tribe of the Sunflower Family has flowers that are terminal and solitary up to one and a half inches wide; the tiny disk flowers are yellow with readily visible black anthers. Both the ray and disk flowers are fertile, making lots of seeds. The leaves are rough, hairy and somewhat glandular and the plants vary from four to sixteen inches tall.

Tidy tips and several other species of layia have long been grown at botanic gardens and are excellent for home gardens, requiring no special treatment. Seed can be broadcast in autumn, just before the soaking rains if possible, since the natural moisture seems to aid in their germination which will probably take two weeks. The area to be planted should be weeded and lightly cultivated first. After sowing, rake the seeds in gently and go over the patch with the back of the rake to be sure the seed is in firm contact with the soil.

Layia is named for D.T. Lay, a botanist who visited California in 1827, 22 years before the gold rush. Wouldn't it have been grand to see our natural landscapes with him? Platyglossa means flat tongue (for the ray flowers).

PHACELIA—*Phacelia* **spp.**

These lovely and ubiquitous spring flowers vary in color from purple to blue to white and even yellow and there are as many as 23 species in each county so we will stay generally with members of the genus that you'll come upon in your peregrinations among the coastal mountains and inland valleys. You will find phacelia in bloom from February to July. We can feel comfortable with these members of the Waterleaf Family because we already are on friendly terms with yerba santa, fiesta flower and baby blue eyes. Phacelias are perennials and mainly herbaceous with stems erect or spreading. The leaves are mostly pinnate or compound. The pretty flower, on a hairy spike-like coil, has a five-parted calyx and a flaring five-lobed corolla. The five stamens are attached near the base inside the tube, and they often extend well above the petals. The style is divided at the top and the fruit develops below it. The seeds in the mature fruit may be pitted or corrugated or neither depending upon which phacelia you're looking at under a lens.

The name is Greek: phakelos—a cluster of crowded flowers. *P. viscida*, a handsome bright blue flower which bloomed widely after the March miracle rains in 1991, was collected in Purisima Canyon by P. A. Munz in 1943. He also collected *P. divaricata* in 1930 on Santa Rosa Island. I am perhaps most impressed by his getting onto that island, which I never have, nor have many others. It is privately owned and is reported to have many natural areas, though long a working ranch. Perhaps Nature Conservancy will make one of their deals and we can go tippy-toe in spring while I'm still able to land off a rocking boat!

BABY BLUE EYES—*Nemophila menziesii*

This quintessential spring wildflower with the sentimental name is widespread in California. Its sky-blue saucer-shaped flowers rise from weak sprangly stems and deeply lobed leaves. This close relative of fiesta flowers may be found in oak groves and around the edges of grassy meadows, scrub and chaparral. Those pictured were growing lustily between a fence and a plowed field in Santa Barbara County (see page C-20).

10
4-16-07

Easy to grow from seed, my first after-school class at the Santa Ana Botanic Garden in Claremont raised them in "their" bed and a tray of paper cups to take home to bloom. We put a fine mesh chicken wire over the bed to keep birds from having our seeds for breakfast. Long in cultivation in Europe, I saw in Holland the biggest bluest baby blue eyes growing in thick rows of a seed catalog company garden plot. Here in Morro Bay they do well in my flower boxes under the west windows. The birds don't find them up there and I readily see if they need weeding or a drop or two of saved rainwater.

BIRD'S EYE GILIA—*Gilia tricolor*

Flowers are pale lavender to deep blue-violet with purple spots at the top of the yellow throat. Sometimes dark color shows on the outside of the floral tube as well. The finely dissected basal leaves are soft and feathery. Found on the eastern open slopes and plains of our area in early spring, this dainty beauty is perhaps extending its geographic range by doing well in wildflower mixes. Recently several lusty plants from a Moon Mountain Wildflowers seed packet grew a good 18 inches high and even hung down over the edge of my window boxes, blooming extravagantly from February well into summer.

ELEGANT CLARKIA—*Clarkia unguiculata*
FAREWELL-TO-SPRING or GODETIA—
Clarkia amoena

Of all the beautiful spring wildflowers none are more handsome than these, whether by the grassy fieldful, on bluffs or up close lying on the ground among them. I remember them from the early 1930s when I found their old name, godetia, in the Richfield color folders. They are called clarkias now, which need not weigh heavily on us flower lovers, but needs to be remembered if one wishes to learn more. There are many species in our three counties and the whole state. Due to their appeal, they are common in gardens and a huge series of cultivars has been developed by hybridization. After considerable mumbling over the literature we came up here with two which have excellent drawings and you'll find another in our Foothill Woodland chapter.

Elegant Clarkia

Elegant Clarkia—*C. unguiculata*—may be found in late spring when drying slopes are brightened by its spidery blossoms. Stems are usually white and smooth, one to three feet tall. The sepals are reflexed and purplish. The pink to lavender petals have narrow bases, often called claws. The stamens are topped by scarlet anthers (see photo on page C-21). The genus name is after Captain William Clark of the 1803 Lewis and Clark Expedition from St. Louis to the Pacific Ocean, and the species name means clawed. Elegant clarkia's nutritious seeds were gathered in quantity by Native Americans to make pinole (soup).

Farewell-to-Spring

Farewell-to-spring or **Godetia**—*C. amoena*—has petals as broadly rounded as elegant clarkia's petals are narrow. Each of the four petals are fan shaped, only gradually narrowing to the base. Farewell-to-spring's colors (all lovely) may be lavender, pink or lavender splotched or penciled with red. I like to remember them as baby pink and suspect the splotches and pencilings are due to our never-ending desire to "improve" on nature. See page C-20 for another godetia-type clarkia called wine cups—*C. speciosa*, which is common in the Monterey-San Luis Obispo-Santa Barbara region.

THISTLE SAGE—*Salvia carduacea*

With its fringed lavender petals and Chinese-red anthers, thistle sage commonly grows along roadsides and out into meadows in the interior. The dense flower heads are surrounded below by spiny bracts and the gray-green foliage is covered with fine hairs and edged with spiny projections, showing its adaptation to the dryer climate here. (I admit to a strong preference for this sage, partly because I pocketed its seed years ago and scattered them behind a rock wall we'd just built, where they grew and reseeded for many springs!)

MARIPOSA LILY—*Calochortus* spp.

These lovely butterfly-flowers vary in color all the way from white through lavender and yellow to rose and red. But you can tell it from the other lilies because its sepals are unlike the petals in shape and color; the flowers are erect on individual stems and usually have a conspicuous gland on the three petals which appears as a bulge on the outside and has hairs and different color areas around it on the inside. The three-parted stigma sits atop the three-sided ovary without a style.

Along the Mt. Abel road and in Lockwood Valley in the southeast back country of this book's area, we have found, in late May to June, a startling red mariposa lily, which will make your day special also when you find it. May we suggest that you get down on your knees in a worshipful position, relax, breathe freely, take pictures and then quietly tiptoe away!

Various members of the genus calochortus use "mariposa" as a common name as well, but don't let it bother you. We are happy flower lovers, nothing more!

OBISPO MARIPOSA—*Calochortus obispoensis*

This lovely lily has deep yellow petals so heavily fringed with bright hairs that one may overlook the three purple-brown petal-tips. The whole flower opens flat, atypical for other mariposas, and three narrow inconspicuous sepals stick stiffly out below and between the petals.

This lily occurs only in San Luis Obispo County and is the logo for the local chapter of the California Native Plant Society. Look for them in late May and early June on dry grassy hillsides often around serpentine rock outcrops. It is an example of an endemic plant that intrigues scientists and flower lovers as well. Why does it grow here and nowhere else? California has quite a few endemics and as yet no easy explanations. June 5, 1991, will always be a memorable day for me. George Benner and I went up on Bowden's Hill—right in the city of San Luis Obispo—and counted 22 of these really handsome lilies among the tall grass, serpentine rocks, prickly pear cactus and abundant (and also yellow) bloomeria. I had seen just one obispo mariposa in bloom in nature before in my long lifetime!

In July of 1991, to my delighted surprise, one bloomed in my yard. No, I did not dig it up in the wild, a bulldozer did, in the hills east of Prefumo Canyon in San Luis Obispo. Our Wednesday hikers group just happened along quite soon after and we gathered up a few tiny bulbs lying "ravished" in the cleat tracks. Mine all turned out to be wild onions—alliums—except for one droopy dwarf that grew slowly, branched a little and developed three tiny buds. They were obispo mariposas.

SCARLET BUGLER—*Penstemon centranthifolius*

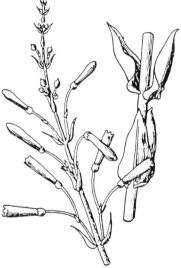

This neat erect wildflower is in the same family and genus as the blue penstemons and is a perennial scattered in sandy or rocky places in the hills of the interior parts of our area and blooms April through July. Though seldom plentiful you'll find them along back country roadsides and cleared areas like firebreaks. Scarlet bugler's flowers come up out of the opposite bracts above the large attractive clasping leaves on one to three foot tall stems; the red tubular corollas slope downward for the convenience of—you guessed it—hummingbirds! While the plant is herbaceous you may find some with a woody base, the leaves are all smooth edged and the red corollas are an inch or more long. Scarlet bugler is highly desirable as a garden plant. So if you have space, sun and coarse soil, why not give it a try? Marjorie Schmidt says in her excellent *Growing California Native Plants*, "Neat, self-contained, free flowering and adaptable to garden culture for semi-dry borders and dry slopes." They make lots of seed and can be propagated from seed without pretreatment. Sow the seed in a flat in the late fall and keep just damp between rains. Young vigorous plants should be individually potted in gallon cans and then set out in the garden after several months.

WILD ONION—*Allium* spp.

Like cultivated ones, all forty-odd California wild onion species smell, often strong, sometimes garlicky. They are usually a foot or more tall. The flowers are rose-purple or lighter colors with darker mid veins. Both leaves and bulbs are edible and were widely used by Native Americans. Onion leaves are all basal, and the flowers are all at the tip of the stem in one fairly loose cluster (umbel) beneath which are one to several papery bracts. The flower sepals and petals (three each) are usually free from each other. The inner petals often have wavy or crimped edges and are shorter than the outer sepals which are longer, wider and smooth-edged. Alliums are in the Liliaceae Family. Wild onions are scattered on both sides of the coastal mountains in our three counties and in several communities. You stand a good chance of finding onions in bloom from March to May most years.

My Wisconsin grandmother taught me to recite for her (when I was too young to object) at her Thursday Literary Society meeting, these lines:

> *"Oh, would some Burbank of the west*
> *Invent, or make, or sell—*
> *An onion with an onion taste,*
> *But with a violet smell."*

BLADDER POD—*Isomeris arborea*

Here we have a different but interesting evergreen shrub that has a strange distribution pattern. Formerly common on sea bluffs and in coastal scrub, it now is scattered in the dry interior valleys of San Luis Obispo and Santa Barbara Counties and the high deserts farther south and east.

The yellow flowers are in terminal clusters. The corolla is two-lipped, consisting of four petals up to an inch across, with stamens extending well out beyond the petals. The leaves are yellow-green to grayish and divided into three leaflets, releasing a strong unpleasant scent only if crushed. The much-inflated long-stalked seed pods are one to two inches long and persistent.

I suggest isomeris, with its long blooming period, evergreen foliage and large attractive pods, be considered for your native garden if you have enough room. It prefers well drained soils and is drought tolerant, once established. In nature they bloom from March to June. At Rancho Santa Ana Botanic Garden, flowers and pods were found on bladder pod at any time of the year, and received much favorable

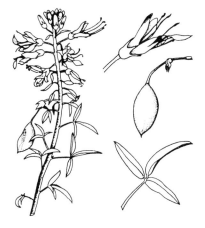

comment from visitors. I have been occasionally asked what the "purpose" or selective advantage of the inflated pods might be. I wish I knew. One imaginative but somewhat logical idea is that, since these shrubs evolved in arid climates, seed dispersal would be aided as the light weight and buoyant pods could ride far down a wash on the flash floods for which desert areas are notorious.

7. FOOTHILL WOODLAND

INTRODUCTION TO THE COMMUNITY

The area covered includes the eastern base of the Santa Lucia Range, the Salinas River drainage and the western slope of the Gabilan Range, borders both sides of the La Panza Range, is also weakly represented in the upper Arroyo Grande Valley and Cuyama Canyon and goes south along the Sierra Madre Range and further south along the Santa Inez and San Rafael Ranges. Typical trees are live oak, gray pine, blue oak, California bay, and occasional groups of buckeye trees. Mottled slopes of intervening or understory chaparral are as characteristic of this community in the interior Coast Ranges as are the trees. Most of the herbs found in this community are also found in grassland areas, but there they probably are relics from a time before trees were cleared away.

Elevations of 400 to 3000 feet are found, and the foothill woodland community fingers upward on warm slopes to 5000 feet mainly on east slopes of the Coast Ranges in all three counties. Hot dry summers with little fog is typical of the climate, with winter rainfall averages of 15 to 40 inches.

A relatively undisturbed example of foothill woodland may be seen by driving along the Nacimiento-Fergusson Road from Jolon westward through the Fort Hunter-Liggett Military Reserve.

BLUE OAK—*Quercus douglasii*

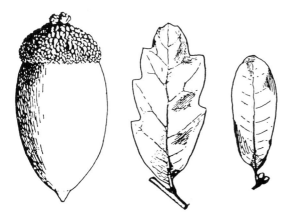

A small or medium size deciduous tree, blue oaks grow 20 to 60 feet tall and have short stout branches that usually form a rounded crown. Not at all shade tolerant, blue oaks often grow with gray pines or in almost pure stands on dry rocky slopes below 3500

feet on the inner sides of the Coast Ranges in all three counties. Bark on the trunks is light gray, thin and narrowly ridged and flakes off easily. The blue-green color of the foliage gives this drought-tolerant tree its common name. Up close the leaves are actually blue-green above and yellow-green beneath and extremely variable in form and size; however, look for shallow lobes or notches or perhaps a few unequal teeth! Blue oaks dangle their little catkins just before or with the opening of the leaf buds in spring. Like other oaks they are prolific periodic producers of acorns which usually ripen in September.

I have had the good fortune to go hiking several times in early April in the ranges bordering both sides of the Cuyama Valley when these hardy little trees were just leafed out, grasses were freshly sprouted and both white and rose-violet shooting stars were blooming. These memories cause me to wonder how some people can say that we have no seasonal change in California!

GRAY (formerly DIGGER) PINE—*Pinus sabiniana*

As children, we usually envisioned pine trees as tall, narrow, single-trunked triangles. Gray pines, however, often have forked trunks with spreading and irregular crowns. They grow 40 to 80 feet tall with seven to 13 inch long needles in bundles of three. Tree trunks from 20 to 24 inches in diameter are 40 to 50 years old. Their clusters of large cones look from a distance like so many perched crows. The heavy cones mature by September of the second year and remain on the tree several years. The cone scales open slowly so seeds are shed over several months. Gray pine seeds are about three-quarters of an inch long, larger than most pine nuts, have short wings and are dark brown. They seed annually, with cones more abundant some years than others. Seeds germinate late in the rainy winter season on bare mineral soil. They grow thriftily on dry, shallow, coarse, gravelly soil, which is often baked and cracked through hot rainless summers.

These hardy pines seem unaffected even when nearby brush is killed by drought. They grow singly, in open groups or widely scattered, mostly with chaparral and foothill oaks.

I had seen gray pines scattered about in the past, but I never really appreciated them until I read *An Island Called California* by Elna Bakker and learned that their different growth habit is an evolving adaptation to where they live. Now when I seen them along the road to Atascadero in summer, for instance, "sifting the intense sunlight through their thin gray long-needled foliage," I nod with respect and find a new beauty in their silhouettes.

The large seeds were an important food source to Native Americans. Early settlers who migrated westward observed these first people digging bulbs for food and called them "digger Indians." Later they saw them gathering the large nutritious nuts under gray pines and named this strange-to-them pine after their name for the first people. It was an unfortunate put-down and only exposed the ignorance of the settlers from the east about the many adaptive skills of these indigenous people who had lived here successfully for thousands of years without negative impact on the environment. Then our culture, with its arrogant attitudes, European diseases and ever-increasing numbers, decimated the Native Americans and their old ways and still seems determined to destroy the land, water and air on which we all depend.

An article in the spring 1992 issue of *News from Native California*, called "A Pine Nut By Any Other Name..." by Leanne Hinton, was most encouraging. She described a Miwok Indian action whereby a group of native people burned "Old Man Digger" in effigy. The Miwoks danced and chanted in joy that a hated name was passing. The article stated that "Native Americans are openly questioning racist terms now, and this is having an important impact on public opinion.... It is time and far past time that the...offensive term "digger" be removed from common botanical nomenclature. This must of course be removed by a grass-roots movement; common names are not regulated by any administrative or scientific authority; the best we can do is refuse to use a given term in print and in voice, and always use another instead."

Leanne Hinton suggests several possible names. The idea I like best is "to call it by a name originally given to it in...Native Californian languages. A name like Towani Pine (Maidu) or Nayo Pine (Wappo) would sound especially lovely." (I vote for Towani Pine!) You might like to join the grass-roots movement as I shall by writing to: Leanne Hinton, Associate Professor, Linguistics Department, University of California, Berkeley, CA 94720.

BUCKEYE or HORSE-CHESTNUT—*Aesculus californica*

This handsome small tree (to 40 feet) is broad-crowned, deciduous and has large thin green palmate leaves. The smooth gray-white bark stands out against its darker neighbors.

The large spikes have showy white flowers and orange anthers. The petals are tinged with rose or yellow. The flower spikes stand out conspicuously from the tree. All of the blossoms on the spike are pollen bearing; usually those at the top of the cluster are bisexual and the only ones producing fruit. They usually bloom April through June. The lifestyle of this beautiful tree is unique among California trees as far as I know. They come into leaf in March; by July and August the leaves wither and soon drop off. The fruits, which are small and immature when the leaves fall, continue to develop through the summer and, by late fall, the leafless tree is adorned with large tan pear-shaped fruits which later split to reveal a shiny red-brown seed. This seed appearing through the opening capsule is probably the basis for the common name, i.e. buck's eye.

Our western horse-chestnut is common on dry slopes and canyons below 4000 feet in Monterey County and north. In our other two counties most trees are assumed to be planted and then reproduce spontaneously. Munz' *A California Flora*, however, lists them in north Los Angeles County and Kern County. It is thought that the present distribution of buckeye trees was probably affected by the geographical patterns of Native American use. The trees are frequently found near kitchen midden mounds. Buckeye seeds were used by some early dwellers here to stupefy fish in temporarily dammed up streams. Native Americans knew how to make the large fleshy but toxic nuts edible, in ways rather similar to acorn processing. They were steamed for several hours until the consistency of a boiled potato. Then they were mashed and leached for several days in a stream. This treated starchy material was eaten cold or made into cakes. Buckeye meal did not keep very well, so early people would have family gatherings and processing parties and throw a feast or "Big Time.".

One final footnote on this remarkable tree that has taken a different route to survival over time in changing climates and associates. Rancho Santa Ana Botanic Garden originated in 1927 in the canyon of the same name. In 1951 the botanic garden was moved to Claremont and the original site abandoned. For 26 years the plants left behind received no care and only natural rainfall. In 1977 a survey was made to see what species might still be growing. It was thought this information would be of value, i.e. what survived in Orange County without irrigation or care. About 45 buckeyes were found growing on a steep west-facing slope in excellent condition. *California Native Trees and Shrubs* quotes Dick Tilforth as saying of this find, "The finest specimens of this species I have ever seen, 46 years old."

INLAND BLUE LARKSPUR—*Delphinium patens*
RED LARKSPUR—*Delphinium nudicaule*

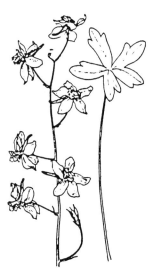

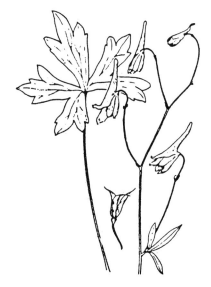

Inland Blue Larkspur   *Red Larkspur*

It's always nice to find larkspurs on the grassy hills and among the parklike oak woodlands in the spring. The spur, of course, figures importantly in pollination which B.J.D. Meeuse says is done for most larkspurs by bumblebees. I've not yet seen it happening but have watched them working monkshood, a close relative, in the mountains, and assume the foraging strategies are similar, i.e. the bumblebee pushes in under the petals and anthers, over the stigmas and beyond to reach the nectar at the bottom of the spur. Whether the bee both collects pollen and delivers it with one trip remains to be learned. The more we find out, the more questions arise! We do know that bumblebees are more individualistic than honeybees and that some flowers require them to buzz while inside, to get the pollen to fall out of the anthers onto their backs! Won't it be fun next spring to sit quietly near some larkspur to see what we can discover?

Larkspurs are well known garden plants. From some thirty California natives we chose three beautiful representatives for our three counties, and put them all in this book—two in this community and one you've already seen (*Delphinium parryi* ssp. *blochmaniae*) in Chapter 2, Beach Dunes. Many larkspurs are poisonous to cattle and horses that may eat them in early spring before the grass is well up; sheep are seldom affected. Larkspurs have five brightly colored sepals, the upper one forming the spur. They have four inconspicuous petals, numerous stamens and three pistils.

Inland blue larkspur—*D. patens.* This one represents all the various southern blues of our area. Patens refers to the spreading tips of the three-parted fruits. The four sepals are long and spreading and the fifth sepal or spur is rather short. This purple-blue beauty blooms on moist slopes away from the coast in the semishade of woods and chaparral in May.

Red larkspur—*D. nudicaule.* This bright red lovely is two feet tall, has leaves that are hairless, thick and with wide blunt segmented lobes. The sepals and long spur are the showy parts, the petals are inconspicuous and yellowish, sometimes tipped with red. It is found in Monterey County back from the coast and north, and blooms from March to June on rocky moist slopes in partial shade. Another scarlet larkspur, *D. cardinale*, is found from Monterey County south. It is taller, three to six feet high. Its basal leaves wither early, giving it the look of a long leafless panicle of spurred flowers. This one can be found in open dry places among chaparral and woodland, beginning to bloom in May.

YELLOW PANSY or WILD VIOLET or JOHNNY-JUMP-UP—*Viola pedunculata*

These fragrant flowers are every flower lover's delight most springs from February to April. In California there are some 25 species that differ widely in color and leaves. Wild violet commonly grows on grassy slopes below 2500 feet in elevation in all three of our counties. This yellow flower's petals usually have some brown on their backs and brown streaks in the throats of the lower ones. Johnny-jump-ups have woody roots, stems four to fourteen inches tall and leaves one to two inches long (not heart-shaped) on stems one to three inches long. The flower-stalks (peduncles) are four to six inches long. This species' name tells us that these features distinguish this yellow pansy from the many others.

DOUGLAS WALLFLOWER—*Erysimum capitatum*

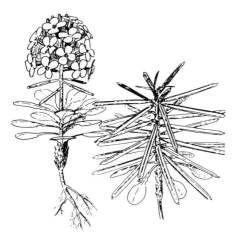

These clusters of bright yellow-orange, four-petaled, sometimes fragrant flowers top one to two-foot erect stems. The basal leaves are narrow, irregularly toothed, rough-hairy and gray-green. The inch or more long seed pods are narrow, erect and typical of one branch of the large and lusty Mustard Family. The seeds are welcome food for small birds and mammals. This family is useful to us two-legged mammals as well i.e.: radishes, Brussel sprouts, cabbage and all its horticultural manipulations like broccoli and cauliflower. The latest I've tried is cauli-brocc; it looks like cauliflower but is yellow-green instead of white. Perhaps a tad more Vitamin A. ¿Quien sabe? There is probably one or more wallflowers in all our communities, but we include *E. capitatum* because it is so readily found scattered on dry wooded or rocky slopes and often in disturbed places. It blooms from March well into June and July. Pictured here is a related species, *E. menziesii*.

See Marjorie Schmidt's *Growing California Native Plants* for easy culture from seeds: "Although a biennial, Douglas wallflower is inclined to persist for several years and provides volunteer seedlings."

My first personal recollection of wallflower goes back to the time I'd just acquired a macro lens for my camera, and "drama in real life" came zooming up through it, right away. A wee little fly-like insect was busily going about on the bright yellow, half inch flowers, when out from under came a little bright yellow crab spider, who lunged and caught the fly and began to devour it. All this went on in a half inch cube of space! I trust you can well imagine the pictures I took. If the fly was in focus the spider was fuzzy and in all of them the flower was a yellowish blur! Ever since when I see wallflower I nod knowingly because I'm aware that just growing prettily along rock walls is not its whole life experience!

MINER'S LETTUCE—*Claytonia* (formerly *Montia*) *perfoliata*

This small rather succulent annual herb has tiny white flowers. So why is it in this book? Because of its numerous round relatively large leaves that catch your eye, and it is useful. Claytonia's lower leaves are narrow and/or spatulate, but its upper larger leaves form a disk around the stem on which the flowers arise. The tiny flowers and buds nestle in the bottom of the concave disk on new plants. This

tender green plant may be found February through May in shaded and moist places under spreading oak trees and also in chaparral and coastal scrub.

Native Americans ate the tender fleshy leaves raw or cooked and made a tea of the whole plant to use as a laxative. Miners ate the leaves—a source of Vitamin C—to help prevent scurvy.

The black, shiny seeds are an important food source for songbirds and the kangaroo rat, which eats the leaves as well. A tasty salad can be made by adding claytonia's stem leaves, before the flowers develop, to other veggies and seasonings. C.B. Clarke suggests adding a tangy ingredient as she finds it rather bland by itself. (I suggest adding sliced wild radish seed pods which provide a nip.) Often on day hikes I've opened my sandwich and added several leaves of miner's lettuce for their pleasant fresh crunchiness. Apply the practical Girl Scout rule; "if there are nine or more plants in a square yard, take one for further learning." Remember it's an annual plant—if we eat too many there won't be much seed for next year.

FOOTHILL PENSTEMON or BEARD TONGUE—*Penstemon heterophyllus*

I met this penstemon since retiring to Morro Bay, but have some memorable friends among this large genus from my backpacking summers in the Sierra Nevada Mountains. Approaching an 11,000 foot pass into northern Yosemite we came upon the most beautiful blue flowers spilling out of a granite crevice that I had ever seen. There in that high, wild, elemental place they looked as if a skillful Japanese gardener had grown them in a flower box. I shall always treasure the memory of that sight.

Since then I have had love affairs with pride-of-the-mountain (rose-violet) and the fuzzy-all-over foxtail penstemon. But let's return to the now world and enjoy foothill penstemon which is probably the most widespread species in California. It has a woody base, grows one to one and one half feet high with narrow leaves and bears clusters of violet flowers with blue lobes. The undeveloped buds are yellow. The open two-lipped corolla (two lobes above, three below) has four stamens curving up around the side of the mouth like dragon's teeth, plus the fifth sterile stamen (the beard tongue) curving up into the top center ready to spread pollen from the fertile ones around on the bee or hawk moth which comes for sips of nectar. (It takes a lot of empathy to imagine giving up sex to do that!)

In other words, the fifth stamen is elongate and flattened and in many species bristly like an old toothbrush. It mechanically aids in distributing pollen from the other fertile anthers over the insect's furry body. This species grows on dry hillsides below 5000 feet and begins to bloom in April.

I have grown *P. heterophyllus* in my yard and also the hybrids P. Fireball and P. Midnight. See scarlet bugler for garden culture hints.

GLOBE GILIA—*Gilia capitata*

Capitata means headed and this species of gilia does indeed have round, tight flower clusters. The corolla tube is not over 1/8 of an inch across and 1/4 to 3/8 inch long. There may be fifty to 100 flowers per head. Usually the flower color is sky-blue, though color does vary. The stamens are longer than the corollas. These lovely annual wildflowers grow one to three feet tall, branch at the base or above and have dissected leaves. They are found in the Santa Lucia Range, eastward and south through the inner coast ranges. There are many subspecies which are not confined to foothill woodland, but are well represented in this community. They usually bloom from March into June .

I shall always remember with joy a sunny spring day at the botanic garden in Claremont when a group of first and second graders sat on the path around a bed of wild flowers in full bloom. They were "bee watching," which they'd done before, when one young man announced gravely that his bee had blue pollen baskets. Various adults including a grad student came around to see and sure enough, George's bee was working globe gilia flowers and its pollen baskets were blue. I've since observed that most of the various gilias do have blue pollen in their anthers. Then I remember George and imagine that he's grown up to be a scientist who uses careful observation plus lots of high tech in his research. Of course I like to think that his twig was bent at any early age in our program!

RED RIBBONS—*Clarkia concinna* (also *Clarkia cylindrica* and *Clarkia bottae*)

This queen of the semi-shaded, mostly wooded slopes is a treat to find if you get out and walk along graded back country roads in late spring. Concinna means neat or well made, and red ribbons is a truly bizarre beauty, as well. The stems are reddish, one half to two feet tall. The long narrow red sepals curve back under the rose-pink petals which are up to one inch long. These petals are deeply lobed (the red ribbons) and three spread up and out, while the fourth petal points down. The four stamens and pistil are rather inconspicuous, but they do their share very well. I know because I planted them in my window boxes (a seed packet from Moon Mountain Wildflowers) and they have kept coming up below in the yard for several years. If the first and second leaves of seedlings have a reddish mid-vein, they can be recognized as clarkia seedlings and spared when weeding.

Two other clarkias (godetia style) are: *C. cylindrica*, a delicate plant with wiry stems and red at the bases of the petals. It may be found in scattered colonies on banks, along roads and trails of inland woodlands in Santa Barbara County. *C. bottae* has pink or lavender petals with white bases. This species of clarkia is endemic on the north section of the Monterey Peninsula and the Santa Lucia Mountains, mainly near the coast, but is probably now found mostly in cultivation.

CHINESE HOUSES—*Collinsia heterophylla*

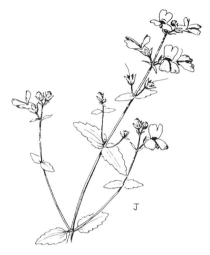

This dainty annual wilding may be found scattered about in colonies in cool shady woodlands, on north slopes in coastal chaparal and inland along shady roadsides and grassy slopes. The flowers are indeed spaced up the stems in one to five whorls like Chinese pagodas. They bloom from March into June. The beautiful two-lipped corollas may be white, pink, rose or purple with the lower three-lobed lip usually deeper in color. The erect upper lip is cleft, while the middle of the lower lip is boat-shaped, enclosing the style and four stamens. The upper pair of stamens have short up-turned basal horns. Stems are one half to one and a half feet tall and the leaves are opposite with the upper blades triangular. There are many other species of collinsia but *C. heterophylla* is most frequently found in our area. Chinese houses are in the Figwort Family which gives us lots of colorful spring wildflowers as well as garden favorites like penstemons, monkey flowers, snapdragons and foxgloves.

Purple Chinese houses can be grown from package seed broadcast in autumn and again in early spring to extend the blooming period. When well established and allowed to seed, it will volunteer plants and form nice colonies. They require high broken shade, as under trees, regular moisture and a little humus in the soil. They are appropriate in a cool border, massed around trees and in a shaded rock garden or mixed flower border.

SHOOTING STARS—*Dodecatheon* spp.

These flowers are rose-violet, occasionally white, and may be found in early spring in grasslands and open woods. Shooting stars are numerous in wet years, but findable in dry ones in small clumps or in the lee of a "meadow muffin." Hanging upside down with recurved petals, how do these lovelies get pollinated? Get comfortably stretched out in the sun some March afternoon and watch the winged nectar and pollen seekers. You'll discover several fascinating things about this flower, the insects and, perhaps, yourself! Soon after pollination, the flower's stem turns upward and the seed pods are erect when they open. I've found dry, open pods rattling in a windy pass, dropping seeds into snow to be widely distributed at melt time.

GOLDFIELDS or SUNSHINE—*Lasthenia* (formerly *Baeria*) *chrysostoma*

This small but numerous "sunflower" grows up to six inches high and often carpets acres of thin soil in the foothills and interior valleys with vegetative sunshine in spring. This most ubiquitous species was named *L. chrysostoma* or golden mouth, for the disk flowers. Goldfields have narrow opposite leaves; they are annuals which begin making a year's seed crop in March and can still be found blooming into May in years of ample rainfall. Our drawing shows *L. macrantha*, a close relative from the coast.

INDIAN PAINTBRUSH—*Castilleja* spp.

Widespread, pretty and usually findable most anytime of the year, paintbrushes bloom heavily in spring. The <u>real</u> flowers are small, green-tipped and rather tubular; they peek out of the highly colored bracts and upper leaves that surround them and attract hummingbirds and flower-lovers. The relationship of flower parts and colors is similar to the familiar poinsettia plant. To be sure you've found the true flower, look for the tiny knobbed pistil sticking out of the top. Paintbrushes vary in color from pale yellow through orange to bright red. Since color is not usually the basis for classification, they are all castillejas and which species is at hand is beyond the scope of this book. This plant is semi-parasitic, manufacturing only part of its food in its slender green leaves. Its roots grow through the soil until they touch roots of other plants, usually a woody-based shrub, where they penetrate the tissues of the host and take part of its food.

8. STREAMSIDE WOODLAND

INTRODUCTION TO THE COMMUNITY

Streamside or riparian woodland as this community is often called is represented by trees, shrubs and herbs that are restricted to the banks of rivers, streams (including intermittent ones), seasonal trickles, springs and fresh water seeps (cienagas). In the streamside woodlands of Monterey, San Luis Obispo and Santa Barbara Counties is found the nearest group of ecosystems comparable to the midwest and eastern United States in terms of plants and, to some extent, weather as well. Cold air settles into our steep narrow and convoluted canyons along water courses. In the winter months when days are short, the vegetation along these streams receives less sunlight than that growing on the ridges, bluffs and shallow inland valleys. Deciduousness is definitely advantageous under these environmental conditions.

Here such trees as sycamore, the cottonwoods, willow, wax myrtle, white alder and bigleaf maple are well represented. Box elder—*Acer negundo*—is often included but we did not, partly because the only place I've seen it growing is over the fence in the doggie-relief area at the roadside rest on Highway 101 near Bradley. It has most of the riparian attributes and is an attractive tree and should be considered by planners for parks and other public landscaping projects where its water requirements can be naturally met.

Many of these plants probably descended eons ago from common ancestors of eastern temperate woodlands—a good place for many of us to visit when feeling nostalgic for our own origins!

In planning a driving trip, riparian vegetation may be found along the Salinas River and some of its tributaries and also along streams flowing directly into the sea as along Highway 1 between San Simeon and Monterey. Farther south, streamside areas are found inland between the Santa Ynez and San Rafael Mountains and upper Cuyama Valley.

WESTERN SYCAMORE—*Platanus racemosa*

One of our most beautiful native trees, sycamores have mottled greenish white bark both on young trunks and on the angular branches of old trees. Irregular sheets of bark are shed annually as the trees grow in diameter. The large bases of old gnarled trees have dull brown bark which is often ridged and furrowed but shed much more gradually. Long lived trees, sycamores, also formerly called "buttonwood" for the pendulous strings of flower and seed balls, grow to 60 feet tall and their long, crooked branches make a picturesque irregular crown. Crowded in deep canyons, some trees reach 75 to 80 feet tall. In such situations they are, of course, vulnerable to battering by rocks, debris and roaring water at times of high rain runoff.

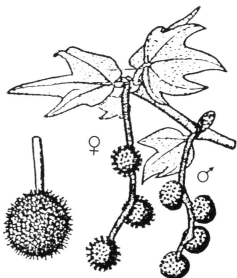

Sycamore's handsome leaves are up to 10 inches long and often still broader. Three to five-veined, lobed mature leaves are green and smooth above, paler and rusty-hairy beneath. Deciduous sycamores are usually the last trees to drop their leaves after turning yellow in November. The flowers are of two kinds; the rosy-red female flower heads are up to an inch in diameter on a single string five to ten inches long. The furry red outside of the buttons are tiny stigmas of many individual flowers. The ovules below these stigmas develop into bristly seed buttons (see the enlarged drawing of one seed-head) and the seeds get about much like dandelions on their "parachutes" and the wind. The other yellow-green smaller buttons that develop on different strings are usually four to six per string; these produce the pollen. The female flowers mature first, receive pollen on the wind from a different tree and begin making seeds before the yellow-green buttons mature. During my early years at the botanic garden in Claremont, I watched this process while waiting for school buses to arrive. The sycamore that grows gracefully by the stone and timber entrance eventually let branches down where the students, returning to the bus, loved to finger-snap the yellow balls to see the little puffs of pollen fly.

Back in our "homesteading" days, I crumbled one seed ball over a dirt-filled gallon can and set it in a pan of water (a method I still use to keep from over-watering potted native plants). I kept the soil damp and yes, they came up like hair-on-a-dog. This is not the happy ending; those little green "whiskers" damped off in a week or ten days. We crumbled another seed button with Rootone powder, they did fine and all our friends and relatives got little sycamore seedlings for Christmas that year! In nature they grow along water courses as they require adequate moisture for good growth; they also tolerate both high temperatures and wind. Beautiful and much admired, sycamores have a place in today's landscaping. Probably they are best suited to large informal gardens, parks and creekside restoration projects in cities. San Luis Obispo has had several such efforts along the creek that winds through this city. Here quite old sycamores have survived that probably were here in Spanish mission days. There are several parks in interior parts of our three counties graced by huge old sycamores, and their summer shade is greatly appreciated.

BLACK COTTONWOOD—*Populus trichocarpa*
FREMONT COTTONWOOD—*P. fremontii*

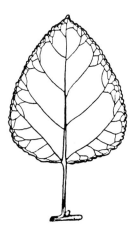

Cottonwoods are called poplars by easterners. Two personal impressions are memorable regarding these common canyon-bottom trees. Driving north up Highway 395 near Little Lake there is a double row of cottonwoods on the west side, planted years ago by a local rancher. I happened along when the seeds were ripe and they with their cotton parachutes covered the highway in deep rolling white fluff. As I drove slowly through, it dawned on me that this is why these trees are called COTTON woods. The other first memory is from my years at the botanic garden in Claremont. A school group and I were "discovering" our way back toward the bus in

Black Cottonwood

the desert area, below the mesa, where the path turns close by a fairly small cottonwood that was just letting down its large colorful pollen catkins all over the tree. The label identified it as a Fremont cottonwood and back in my office the literature told me lots about cottonwoods, but that school group and I had experienced its first blooming close up in the garden's living laboratory.

Black cottonwood is the largest of our western poplars. Its pale gray bark is thick and deeply and regularly furrowed. Its spreading branches form a broad open crown. They were extensively planted by early settlers for shade and wind breaks. The leaves are longer than wide, finely toothed, shiny dark green above, pale green and sometimes rusty below. They have long leaf stems (petioles) which let them move easily in the breeze. However they don't really "quake" like their famous mountain cousin, quaking aspen—*P. tremuloides.* The

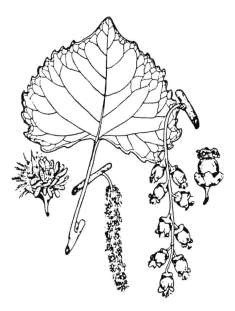

Fremont Cottonwood

leaves turn a dull yellowish-brown as days grow shorter in autumn. Their reddish yellow buds are covered with a fragrant gum from which the tree gets its old name: balsam cottonwood. This tree probably attains the greatest age of all our poplars. A tree 43 inches in diameter showed an age of 112 years when cut down. It is a prolific annual seeder with a high rate of germination, though the seed has a brief vitality life if stored. Reproduction is good on moist bare humus or sandy soils and very abundant on wet sand bars in streams. The largest trees occur at low elevations in river bottoms and permanent creeks. Intolerant of shade, they used to form belts and limited forests of pure growth, but now occur mixed in with alders, big leaf maples and willows. In our three counties black cottonwoods grow along streams near the coast, becoming less numerous inland to the Salinas River drainage and south near Madulce Peak and the upper Santa Barbara Canyon and the Sespe Creek area. Usually found between 500 and 2700 feet in elevation, black cottonwoods bloom in February to April. Their catkins shed pollen to the breeze and then drop to the ground.

Fremont cottonwood is a handsome, generally smaller tree than black cottonwood, with a spreading crown, well-spaced foliage and whitish trunk when young. The bark becomes furrowed, thick and dark gray later. The leaves are yellow-green above and lighter green underneath, long and wide with blunt curved irregularly-toothed margins. Leaf petioles may be up to three inches long, flattened and yellowish. Fremont cottonwood's leaves turn a bright lemon yellow in autumn. This tree is very common in the interior of our area extending into tributaries east of the Salinas River and in canyons like the upper Sespe Creek to the south. Well adapted to moist sandy, gravelly or humus soils, it withstands high temperatures and is extremely intolerant of shade. It grows rapidly where these conditions are met and is probably relatively short lived. After severe floods it comes in with willows, sycamores and white alders, but may be shaded out over time by these taller growing trees. With its relatively small size, yellow fall foliage, colorful catkins and rapid growth, Fremont cottonwood is a valuable tree for parks, along highways and in home gardens with enough room and water, better than the exotic columnar Lombardy poplar which we often see dying along roadways. Once established, both Fremont and black cottonwoods seem to survive protracted drought in nature. Let's try them in ornamental horticulture.

ARROYO WILLOW—*Salix lasiolepis*

(Paraphrased from an article by Dr. Dirk R. Walters in the San Luis Obispo Chapter of the California Native Plant Society newsletter, with approval.)

Anticipating spring and its showy flowers, we may overlook some of the less flamboyant flowers of the winter season. One such flower is that of the common arroyo willow, *Salix lasiolepis*. Individual arroyo willow flowers are certainly nothing to get excited over. They consist of either two stamens or a single pistil hidden in the axil of a somewhat hairy bract. Staminate and pistillate flowers occur on separate plants. The bracts and thus the flowers are aggregated into tight elongated clusters called catkins. In some species of willow, the bracts are so hairy that the catkins give the appearance of the soft hairy covering of a cat's foot and have been given the common name of pussy willows. These especially are appreciated and gathered for bouquets by people not blessed with our ideal climate.

The willow clan is very common and widely distributed throughout the temperate and sub-polar regions of both hemispheres. Their commonness, their ease of propagation from seed or cuttings and their ability to grow under every conceivable condition except dryness have led most of us to consider willows to be nothing but weeds. But to our ancestors they were very valuable. Willows are fast growing and the soft wood is easily worked and burns readily. Willows are of extreme importance in protecting both streams and their banks from excessive erosion and as barriers against floods. Those that grow in the channel slow down stream flow so that run-off is lessened and more of the water can seep into the ground to charge the underground aquifers. The flexible twigs were important to California Indians as a major constituent in their excellent baskets, among many other things.

Hippocrates prescribed willow bark to treat pain and fever. Most if not all willows contain a substance the body converts to a salicylate. In 1853, French chemist Charles Gerhardt synthesized acetylsalicylic acid, but its effectiveness wasn't known until German scientist Heinrich Dreser spread the word in 1899. Soon after, Mr. Bayer made aspirin an essential component in virtually everyone's medicine cabinet.

Look for this shrub in February in our coastal canyons, and try to imagine how your ancestor might have viewed it. As it is today, it was common then, and its uses were ordinary. They probably took it for granted—maybe we shouldn't.

CALIFORNIA WAX MYRTLE—*Myrica californica*

For a long time I thought of this shrubby tree as another kind of willow, but find that it belongs to a very different, mainly tropical family, more resembling a Brazilian flame bush of ornamental horticulture than it does willows. There is only one species in California, where it is found on sand dunes (Nipomo), moist hillsides and coastal canyons from Santa Monica north to Washington. In our area it may now be found mainly in canyon mouths and scattered thinly among willows on the protected side of the dunes. Myrica is a densely branched, ev-ergreen shrub or small tree to 25 feet high with smooth gray or light brown bark. Its leaves are thick, glossy and dark green above, paler underneath, oblóng, nearly entire and narrowing at the base to a petiole. The tiny flowers bloom in March and April and are separate male and female with the female flowers closer to the tip of the branches than the larger clusters of male flowers. The inter-esting clusters of bumpy berry-like nuts mature in September. They are dull white due to the wax covering which conceals the purple color beneath. They were called bayberries by early settlers from Atlantic shores, who boiled down the berries and poured off the wax into candle molds. When we found some bushes in Montaña de Oro State Park in fruit I yearned to try to resurrect this old folkway, but despaired of finding enough berries or get-ting permission from authorities. Maybe some day!

Meanwhile this attractive small tree, with its clean-looking evergreen foliage, its drought and wind tolerance in coastal areas and its clusters of waxy berries which stay on well into winter, has horticultural value. There is a handsome large formal clipped wax myrtle hedge in the demonstration area at Rancho Santa Ana Botanic Garden.

WHITE ALDER—*Alnus rhombifolia*

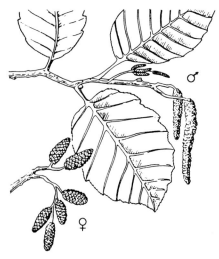

A genus of the Birch Family, these attractive trees with their smooth gray bark and ascending branches grow 40 to 90 feet tall on permanent stream banks of coastal can-yons and inland up into the mountains. The leaves are roughly oval in shape and two to four inches long, green on both sides with fairly flat mar-gins with tiny teeth. White al-der leaves are shed in the fall without much change in color. Male and female flower clus-ters are borne on different parts of the same branch, the males pendant on the branchlet tip. Male catkins elongate up to seven inches. Greenish-yellow in color, they appear before or with the new leaves. In February and

March they produce large quantities of pollen. Lower down on the branch are the much smaller female flowers which develop into three-quarter inch woody "cones." Between the scales of these cones the numerous small flat seeds (nuts) develop. The seeds are usually liberated in midwinter. The library on the second floor of the botanic garden building in Claremont looked out into lovely large alder trees. It was fun at eye-stretching time to watch such birds as ruby crowned kinglets and chickadees picking seeds and perhaps insects out of the cones right at eye level. White alders are fast growers, heat and wind tolerant, but rather short lived. They need a continuous water supply and are susceptible to mistletoe; all of which makes them somewhat doubtful for ornamental planting these days. They are lovely trees in their natural habitat. Soon after coming to live in Morro Bay, some friends and I back-packed up to Cruickshank Camp one clear, dry week in January and explored that wildly beautiful part of the Santa Lucia Mountains. One day we came around a high coastal ridge and looked down into Alder Creek. We ate lunch by the stream in a small grove of mature trees. I can see the tall gray trunks and intricate tracery of bare branches against the blue sky as I remember my first wild stand of white alder trees.

BIG-LEAF MAPLE—*Acer macrophyllum*

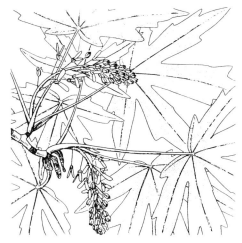

This is one of my favorite deciduous trees and it is always pleasant to see them when hiking in the cool canyons along the coast in all three of our counties. They may also be found scattered inland up to 4800 feet high, especially in the south.

They grow to 60 feet tall with broad crowns and grayish barked trunks to two feet in diameter. The very large leaves are simple and palmately lobed, smooth and green on top, paler underneath, seven to 14 inches wide with six to 12 inch long petioles. Some years they turn a lovely clear yellow before dropping in the early to late fall. The flowers appear in large drooping clusters usually with the first leaves in March to April. Many tree blossoms have few or no petals. Big-leaf maples, however, have true petals, which are fragrant and yellow. Male and female flowers are separate and both can occur on different parts of the same tree.

Big-leaf maple is a handsome tree, alas probably too large for gardens, but suitable for parks where the soil is sandy or gravelly and the water table is not too far down below the surface.

CREEK DOGWOOD—*Cornus californica*

These attractive water-loving shrubs are deciduous in winter which is the best time to see their graceful spreading red-barked branches. Their large green leaves are oval shaped with pointed tips and conspicuous lateral veins. Creek dogwood has rounded clusters of small white flowers in late spring and early summer, followed by round white to bluish fruits (drupes) later in the year. I have a creek dogwood between a shore pine and a large ceanothus on the windy north side of my native garden. It grows and makes suckers in the rather limited space. In the fall of some years the leaves turn a soft rose and yellow for a brief time before falling off. Then I prune it back, take up the suckers (pot some for the plant sale, whence mine came) and bring the lovely red twigs inside for a dry arrangement. It grows naturally in coastal canyons never very far from surface water, but here on the coast in cultivation they tolerate dryness and are not fussy about soil type.

Creek dogwood is not to be confused with mountain dogwood—*C. nuttallii*—whose "flowers" are really four to seven conspicuous white bracts surrounding a tight cluster of small greenish-yellow flowers, somewhat like poinsettias. I grudgingly admit that these small trees are spectacular when in bloom—especially along the road into Yosemite Valley from the Wawona entrance. Mountain dogwood resembles the eastern dogwood—*C. florida*. The latter is easier to grow in cultivation here than *C. nuttallii*, I'm told. Remember they all need water.

TWINBERRY—*Lonicera involucrata* var. *ledebourii*

This attractive upright shrub up to 10 feet tall is frequently found in moist places along the immediate coast from Point Conception north. Its branches are slender and wand-like and densely foliaged with dark green opposite leaves with smooth margins. Yellowish flowers tinged with red grow in pairs on a single stalk coming out of a leaf-axil. The corolla tubes are swollen on one side near the base. These flowers are surrounded by two broad bracts (petticoats) which become quite red when the berries ripen to a shiny black. Both the flowers and fruits make this a delightful discovery along canyon trails from March to July.

This is a good garden shrub, not fussy about soil, drought tolerant, though should have some summer water to look well, withstands temperatures down to 35 degrees F. Flowers and fruit are borne on young shoots, so prune out heavy wood in winter after the leaves have fallen.

SNOWBERRY—*Symphoricarpos mollis*

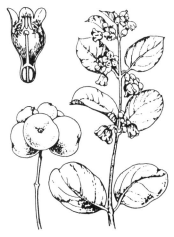

Our last member of the Honeysuckle Family is a low trailing much-branched shrub about 18 inches tall. Its leaves are broad oval to round, softly hairy on both sides, up to three-fourths of an inch long or larger on sterile shoots. The flowers are small, bell-shaped, pinkish white and in pendant pairs in leaf axils or small clusters. They bloom from April to June and off season flowers are commonly found on these bushes. In late summer and fall the large conspicuous white berries appear. One October, as we came up out of the Islay Creek bottom in Montaña de Oro State Park, a swale east of the new loop trail looked like someone had scattered popcorn, until a closer look with binoculars revealed snowberries in rich profusion even after years of drought! Commonly found on lightly shaded slopes in the coast ranges of our three counties, snowberry spreads by suckering, making dense thickets in wet years. This habit makes them useful for bank covers and erosion control. I personally prefer to leave this shrub in wild nature, where they make food and cover for wildlife.

CALIFORNIA BLACKBERRY—*Rubus vitifolius*
WILD BLACKBERRY—*Rubus ursinus*

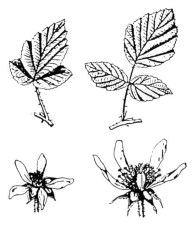

These are evergreen mound builders, trailers or partial climbers, with tip rooting canes as much as 20 feet long. They are quite well known for their straight bristle-prickles. Like the preceding berries, California and wild blackberries are in the Rose Family.

The leaves of *R. vitifolius* are bright green above and lightly hairy beneath; each leaf is deeply three-lobed or divided into separate leaflets with little prickly teeth. The chief difference between these two berry bushes is that *R.*

Wild Blackberry

ursinus has duller leaves, more-or-less felted-woolly beneath.

Blackberries' white flowers are either male or female. The staminate blossoms make pollen and the pistillate ones, after they have been pollinated, make shiny succulent blackberries. (Actually these are compound fruits composed of a number of small fleshy drupelets.) They bloom in March through May or later in steep dark canyons. These berries are edible, tart-sweet and it is hard to find more than a handful at a time. Let's leave most of them for the wildlife.

Both species are widespread throughout much of California, usually in woods or damp riparian situations below 4000 feet in many plant communities. It is generally thought that *R. ursinus* is the progenitor of such cultivated berries as boysenberry, logan-berry, youngberry and olallieberry. Incidentally, raspberries are descended from another close relative—*R. leucodermis*.

WESTERN AZALEA—*Rhododendron occidentale*
CALIFORNIA ROSE-BAY—*R. macrophyllum*

We include these two members of the Heather Family because they are so lovely, though not at all common in our area. George B. Sudworth, who put a wealth of valuable information in his book but gave little space to glowing descriptions, says of these plants, "They are among the most beautiful flowering shrubs and small trees in the world."

Western azalea is a deciduous shrub, loosely branched with shredding bark and thin

Western Azalea

light-green leaves. The handsome white flowers have a salmon-colored area in the middle or have one petal mostly salmon-colored. The slender stamens stand out beyond the petals. These shrubs grow in cool, moist canyons of the coast of Monterey County and also along streamsides in the San Jacinto Mountains and the higher ranges of San Diego County. The first mentioned disjunct population is where I first saw them blooming. Azalea Trails Girl Scout Camp in Dark Canyon, near Idyllwild in Riverside County, was named for this shrub. They generally bloom April to June, later at higher elevations. It is a stellar experience to come around a bend in the trail and find these flowers in shafts of sunlight filtering down through the forest.

California rose-bay will ring bells with gardeners who grow domestic rhododendrons. Their parent stock has long been gathered by horticulturists from all around the world. Its lovely rose-purple blossoms, one to one and one-half inches long, appear in May and may continue to bloom into July. The shrubs vary from four to 12 feet high and have shining dark evergreen leaves two to eight inches long. Found on seabluffs and in shaded woods along the north coast to British Columbia, the Salmon Creek area of Monterey County seems to be its southern geographic limit. I have never seen this beauty in the wild in our area, but still live in hope!

SEEP MONKEY-FLOWER—*Mimulus guttatus*
SCARLET MONKEY-FLOWER—*M. cardinalis*

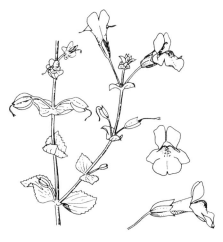

Seep Monkey-Flower

Seep monkey-flower is one of the most widespread species in this large genus of the Figwort Family. The bright yellow flower with red spots on its monkey "face" grows thickly in wet years and produces a few large blooms in temporary wet places in drought years. Look for it also around seeps in coastal bluffs where it blooms March to October. In April of 1983 a large low pasture on the sea side of Highway 1 just south of the culvert at Arroyo de la Cruz near San Simeon was rampant with a seemingly solid cover of these yellow beauties. Closer up these lusty herbaceous plants were seen to be up to two feet tall, rather smooth and producing numerous large blossoms. That spring was the second very wet year of that extensive El Niño period. I watched for them there in subsequent years. There were a few flowers every year until the land was graded and put to producing irrigated row crops, alas. But this pretty and adaptable perennial is not likely to soon become an endangered species. In the fall of 1991 we found some blooming by a lens-shaped pool in the gravelly bed of Chorro Creek near Twin Bridges in Morro Bay!

Scarlet monkey-flower—*M. cardinalis*—is a freely branched, viscid perennial frequent on stream banks and in wet places of our coastal and mountainous canyons. I was able to photograph it in stately profile in a narrow arroyo on Santa Cruz Island, though I remember it being fairly common in the washes coming down off of Mt. San Antonio between Claremont and Upland in early days ago!

BRASS BUTTONS or RANGER'S BUTTONS—
Cotula coronopifolia

This pert little member of the Sunflower Family has a seemingly solid yellow disk which heads up the top of each stem. The outer row of each head is actually made up of ray flowers. Ko-tule is Greek for small cup. This plant's coarse, somewhat succulent alternate green leaves are shallowly and irregularly divided. This bright little low growing weed from South Africa is found scattered about marshy places, ditches and seeps along the coast and inland wet spots in all three of our counties in such "back to nature" locations as Elkhorn Slough in Monterey County, Hazard Canyon in Montaña de Oro State Park and along Alamo Pintado Creek in Birabent Canyon near Ballard campground inland from Santa Barbara. It's very apt to catch your eye most any time of

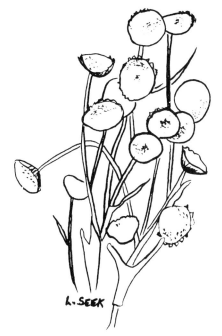

L. SEEK

the year. Though non-native, these bright buttons demonstrate their adaptability by not depending on our chancy rainfall; instead they "know" to grow only in wet places!

POISON HEMLOCK—*Conium maculatum*

This dangerous weed is included here so you may learn to recognize and avoid it. It has many small white flowers and lacy much-divided leaves on two to four foot stalks. The purplish speckles and blotches on the smooth plant stalks are critical in identifying this deadly member of the large and useful Parsley Family, which includes celery—apium, carrots—daucus, anise—pimpinella, Italian fennel—foeniculum, sweet cicely—myrrhis, and cow parsnip—heracleum.

The cup that Socrates

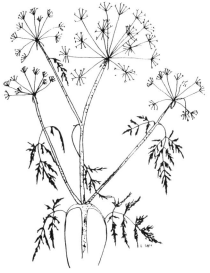

drank to end his life was supposedly made from this plant. A piece of stem the thickness of a pencil and one inch long, if eaten, is a lethal dose. The poison, a volatile alkaloid oil, causes paralysis, loss of muscular control and convulsions, though the mind remains clear until death. Children have suffered toxic effects after using the hollow stems as whistles. This plant grows vigorously in intermittent stream bottoms, covers wide areas, and blooms in the spring.

CRIMSON COLUMBINE—*Aquilegia formosa* var. *truncata*

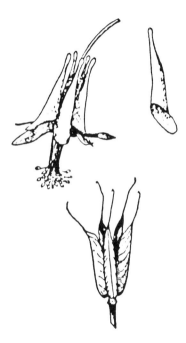

If you have never walked quietly along a sun spangled trail in a forest and paused to watch a hummingbird working columbine, you have a real treat awaiting you. This lovely perennial is widespread but not profuse in moist places about brooks, waterfalls and meadows in our mountains. This species is reported as locally endangered in Santa Barbara County. Columbines have been cultivated in gardens for at least 100 years. The flowers of this species are nodding, scarlet, and the numerous stamens and the petal bases are golden yellow. The ovaries at the bases of the five inconspicuous pistils will develop after pollination into the distinctive seed pods or follicles. Each of the five petals is a long hollow tube (nectar-spur) slanting backwards from the stamens. In between the petal tubes are the petal-like spreading sepals. The leafy stems grow to three feet tall and sometimes branch. The compound leaves have many rounded green leaflets.

FAIRY LANTERN or GLOBE LILY— *Calochortus albus*

Of all of California's wild lilies, I think fairy lantern is my favorite, a real winsome beauty. This species' nodding white globe-shaped bells come also in pink and I have seen yellow ones farther north. Here in our three central coastal counties they are commonly found in cool, moist woodlands. The three petals differ markedly from the three sepals in color and shape (not true of all lilies) and a close look reveals that small hairs line the edges of the petals like a comb. Since fairy lantern petals never open wide, even tiny pollinators must force their way in for a sweet sip of nectar. They probably get well dusted with pollen before they find their way back out through the hair combs. An inside view of one petal (see drawing) shows a nectar gland surrounded by hairs and you'll note when you find them afield that a bump on the outer side of the petal corresponds with the nectar gland within.

The rather large three-sided seed pods are attractive and globe lilies do grow from seeds as well as bulbs. In wet years it is not uncommon to have five lanterns on one stem. Hiking near Salmon Creek one spring, these globe lilies were so numerous that my hiking companion, George Benner, remarked that if we didn't get back before dark the fairy lanterns would help us find our way!

MILK MAIDS or TOOTHWORT—*Dentaria californica*

This pert little member of the Mustard Family—Brassicaceae—used to be called toothwort, now is commonly dubbed milk maids and I'd like to change it to welcome-to-spring, because that's what it does quite early in February. All up and down our coastal counties, it is very apt to be the first herbaceous perennial to open its numerous half inch white flowers along moist canyons and, in wet years, in cool rocky woodlands up some distance from the stream beds.

Like most mustards, the flowers have four sepals, four petals and six stamens (four long ones plus two shorter ones). Below the stigma and style the ovary develops, after pollination, into the long slender seed pod.

Milk maids' leaves are of two kinds: simple and compound; their unbranched stems produce the divided leaves up near the flowers, the lower stem (they grow to 20 inches tall) is bare. The rounded simple leaves come up from an underground tuber or rhizome. So now we find that the genus name means tooth or horn, hence toothwort, and refers to this odd shaped rhizome which used to be eaten raw as a peppery relish. So maybe tooth-wort shouldn't be abandoned as it too is a very basic name, and calls our attention to how the two kinds of leaves originate. Let's not dig up the tubers though, the plants need them more than we need a wild peppery relish!

LEOPARD or TIGER LILY—*Lilium pardalinum*

Large clumps of these beautiful flowers may be found in spring near coastal streams and springs. The three sepals and three petals are so similar we tend to think of these pendant beauties as having six large bright orange recurved petals, with big brownish to maroon spots on them. Six stamens with red anthers attached in the middle to their filaments hang out conspicuously below the petals as does the long yellow style, which has orange-brown stigma knobs. The green strap-like leaves arranged in orderly whorls around the stem are distinctive, too.

These woodland lovelies always remind me of domestic tiger lilies that grew in my aunt's yard in Wisconsin. When my cousins and I played "Indians," we would rub the huge powdery anthers between our fingers and then smear the pollen on each other's faces for "war paint." We sure were pollen wasters back then!

GIANT TRILLIUM—*Trillium chloropetalum*

It's fairly easy to walk by this woodland beauty, but it is really worth spotting. Trilliums grow on stout stems topped with a whorl of three large leaves, usually mottled green, almost as wide

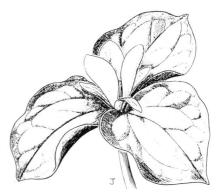

as long. Looking for these leaves is the best way of finding the less conspicuous, perfect solitary flower, which is just above the leaves. The flower color is quite variable but ours are usually deep reddish purple. The three petals are long and narrow with three green sepals outside. In between these petals the six stamens are tall and brownish with linear turned-inward anthers. The female parts produce a round capsule-like berry, which turns reddish with age, and is well filled with seeds. Trilliums are perennial with a large deep rootstock. They grow in colonies and as individuals on moist, shaded woodland slopes, in intermittent-stream canyons and are often associated with poison oak. Trilliums bloom February through April.

We once found the uncommon white trillium—*T. ovatum*—in Julia P. Burns State Park in Monterey County. It differs from our giant trillium more widely found in all three counties in that the leaves are unmottled green. The white triangular petaled flower stands one and one-half inches above the leaves on a stalk or pedicel. This white one reminds me of the common white trillium of my native Michigan.

PURPLE NIGHTSHADE—*Solanum xanti*
BLUE WITCH—*Solanum umbelliferum*

These two sub-shrubs are members of a large genus in the Nightshade Family—Solanaceae—most readily found in our three counties. Blue witch is most often found in Monterey County and purple nightshade in the two southern counties. All are kin to such well known plants as potato, eggplant, belladonna, jimson weed, petunia and also tobacco. The main difference between these two is a fine downiness on the herbage in blue witch, while purple nightshade is seldom

Purple Nightshade

downy. Blue witch is more woody and shrubby, while purple nightshade is mostly herbaceous. Let us flower lovers remember here that hairy fuzz and woodiness are more important in determining species than color. Both of these nightshades have attractive violet-blue or white flowers which are saucer-shaped with fused petals one half inch or more wide. The five erect yellow stamens form a tight group around the tiny greenish style and stigma. The small tomato-like fruits are first green then purple-black when ripe. The flowers often grow in clusters and a few may be found year around in moist woodland areas. The numerous one to three inch long leaves are strong smelling when crushed.

Solanum (Latin "solamem") means quieting, and was used because of the narcotic properties of some species. Nightshade leaves and green fruit are highly toxic, though the ripe berry may be eaten if cooked. Alkaloid poisoning from nightshade results in intestinal distress and/or nervous disorder, sometimes fatal.

But let's not terrify newcomers with the name "deadly" nightshade. It's a common and attractive plant they probably wouldn't eat anyway!

FIESTA FLOWER—*Pholistoma auritum*

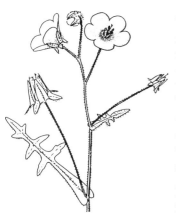

I first found this springtime beauty along the Foxen Canyon Road in Santa Barbara County before I moved to Morro Bay, and have since discovered it in all three counties where it blooms from March into May. This sprawling annual grows in deep canyons and on shaded slopes, frequently under large spreading oak trees. Fiesta flower's stems are two to six feet long, weak and brittle, straggling or climbing by backward pointed prickles over leaf-litter, logs and other plants. The flowers are saucer-shaped to one inch wide and bluish-purple. After a fire, fiesta flowers are conspicuous on the blackened slopes.

We'll end with some Greek and Latin, which you can skip if you wish, or like me, wish you had taken at least one year in high school, because knowing the meaning helps to remember the names of our central coast lovelies. Pholis-stoma means scale mouth, for the corolla tube with five scales. Auritum means small eared, for the clasping lobed leaf bases.

9. REDWOOD/BROADLEAF EVERGREEN FOREST

COAST REDWOOD—*Sequoia sempervirens*

These magnificent trees grow in a narrow strip about 500 miles long and rarely more than 30 miles wide, in a region of frequent summer fog, moderate temperatures and considerable winter rainfall. They do not grow naturally beyond this belt, though I do wish to encourage you to visit the lovely small planted grove at Santa Barbara Botanic Garden. In our three counties, Monterey has the most handsome trees in the State Parks and National Forest along Highway 1. San Luis Obispo County has the dubious distinction of having several canyons on the east side of Highway 1 with dwarfed and blackened redwood groups, demonstrating their remarkable ability to recover after fire!

Coast redwood holds the record for the tallest measured tree species on earth, growing rapidly to more than 360 feet, though average mature trees are about 200 feet high with diameters of ten to 15 feet. Their leaves are short, green, flat and sharp pointed needles. The brown cones are only a half inch in diameter, but produce many tiny seeds.

If redwoods may be said to blossom, it happens in the winter when the tiny male cones cover the outer branchlets mainly up on the crown of the tree. It can be a fine experience when walking the ridge of the Santa Lucia Mountains and gazing upward through the trees to see the golden clouds of pollen drift about on the slightest breeze and realize this has been going on for thousands of years.

Redwoods are adapted to living in flood-prone areas. Following flood deposits, they send temporary roots into the new soil and a new system of surface roots develop from the recently buried trunk base. Redwoods lack a tap root; their massive network of shallow roots enable them to take advantage of fog drip and light summer mists.

Here is an interesting postscript. Rancho Santa Ana Botanic Garden in Claremont has three kinds of redwoods growing there: 1) coast redwood, 2) giant sequoia which grows on the southwest slopes of the Sierra Nevada Mountains, and 3) the dawn redwood, a living fossil from China. Geologically speaking, # 1's fossil record occurs in rocks less than 20 million years old, # 2's to 20 million in a temperate forest, but # 3's history extends back 100 million years into the past when dinosaurs roamed the earth. This tree was known only from its fossil record until after World War II when an enormous tree was noticed in the province of Szechuan in central China. Ralph W. Chaney, a paleontology professor at Berkeley and former president of the Save-the-Redwoods League, journeyed to China to see them. He brought back seed and "my" botanic garden received a share. They look rather like our coast redwoods until autumn when their needles turn yellow and drop off. Whoever heard of a deciduous redwood? I hope you can visit Rancho Santa Ana Botanic Garden someday and see this living fossil for yourself. There are several dawn redwoods planted on the Cal Poly campus in San Luis Obispo as well.

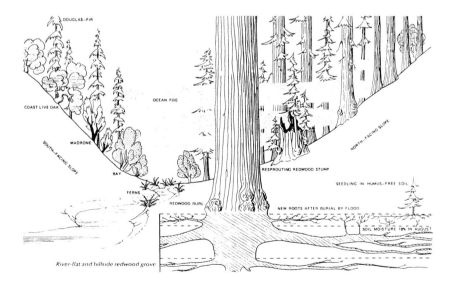

River-flat and hillside redwood grove

PACIFIC MADRONE—*Arbutus menziesii*

A stately tree 60 to 88 feet high with a straight red-brown trunk two to three feet in diameter, it grows in coastal regions from British Columbia to southern California. In our central coast area they are more frequently seen leaning out from steep canyon slopes, 25 to 40 feet high with trunks eight to 15 inches across. Its red-brown trunk, light red branches and large leathery evergreen leaves set it apart from all other trees. It's on the upper stems, limbs and twigs that we see the thin, smooth red bark that peels off in large and small flakes that curl as they dry into two-toned scrolls. On large old tree trunks, the bark is thick, brown and no longer scales off. The pretty little urn-shaped flowers grow in large open-branched clusters showing their kinship to manzanitas (both are in the Heather Family). Look for the translucent "windows" near the bottom of the urn. These are nectaries and are sometimes pierced by "nectar robbers" who, by taking this short cut, fail to aid in pollination. Pollination does occur because madrone trees make lots of berries. A third to a half inch in diameter, orange-red with a finely warty surface, these fruits are eaten by birds who help to distribute the seeds.

The first time I visited the Ventana Wilderness in the Santa Lucia Mountains I was walking along the trail when I heard a fairly loud humming sound and coming around a ridge near Pat Springs, I discovered a large madrone tree in brilliant sunlight and full bloom; it was abuzz with honeybees moving from one inverted white urn to another. The path was covered with shed blossoms. I shall always remember the fecundity of that scene.

Backpacking in the Santa Lucia Mountains in November two years after a forest fire, we saw recovering growth everywhere, but lots of stark blackened trunks, too. The trail from Buckeye Camp to Lion's Den was so open we could see across a canyon where a red-orange haze showed on the other side. Our trail took us around there and we found the color was a heavy crop of Chinese red berries on charred madrone trees. Years later I was to personally discover that madrones crown-sprout after fire. After one Las Pilitas fire on the east Cuesta Ridge in the Los Padres National Forest, we found by the truck trail large madrone burls exposed by the fire-removed duff. The burls had five and six inch sprouts growing lustily up from them. These madrones on Cuesta Ridge have a very different growth habit from the tall woodland trees farther north. Here they grow like their chaparral neighbors on the ridge with many young stems from large old root crowns. I suspect they have experienced numerous fires in their individual lives.

One February, while hiking the Tanbark Trail in Julia Pfeiffer Burns State Park, we found the path sprinkled with madrone berries. As we neared the high ridge, we paused to look out and down and were rewarded with glimpses of the blue sea through the beautiful spreading red branches and wavy green leaves of madrone trees.

"Madrone is very drought tolerant, and thrives in the rocky outcroppings along the tops of coastal ridges. Try a couple in your yard if you have good drainage. They die very quickly in poorly drained or heavy clay soil." —Robert Kowrik in the January/February 1991 issue of *Garbage Magazine*

CALIFORNIA BAY LAUREL or PEPPERWOOD or MYRTLEWOOD—*Umbellularia californica*

This large, handsome evergreen tree belongs to the Laurel Family, which also includes European bay, camphor and our eastern sassafras trees. California bay is commonly found in cool coastal canyon bottoms below 5,000 feet. Inland they occur as shrubs in dry areas. Under most favorable conditions bay trees reach 60 to 80 feet high and two and one-half to three feet in diameter. C.F. Smith describes a huge tree on bottom land along Maria Ignacio Creek in the 1000 block of San Marcos Road in Santa Barbara; it has a spread of over 100 feet. Phillip Wells reports that bay trees will grow high up on slopes containing serpentine. In my own experience, I've found bay trees with large basal burls hanging out over stream banks, sprouting new growth after flood waters recede. Also along east Cuesta Ridge in San Luis Obispo County I've found small but lusty bay trees with large burls which appeared to have crown-sprouted repeatedly after fire. Mature laurel wood is hard and beautiful and takes a high polish, suitable for turning on a lathe. Green unseasoned logs sink in water, where they used to be allowed to soak, producing the formerly popular "black myrtle" wood, which was made into gift items found in shops in northern California and Oregon. The lighter yellow-brown wood seems to be more in style now.

Bay laurel flowers are small but numerous, yellow-green and six to ten per umbel. The fallen petals decorate the ground on trails under bay trees in late winter. Blooming period is from December to May varying with elevation and weather.

The dark green glossy leaves are long and narrow with short stems and are pungently aromatic. When crushed, the leaves give off a light volatile oil. Strong or prolonged sniffs of this oil may cause headaches and nausea in some people. I enjoy the smell of bay leaves and have long gathered a few to use as a spice in soups and stews. If you wish to try cooking with California bay, notice that the flavor is fresher and stronger than that of European bay leaves you've bought in a box, though similar in taste.

The thumb-sized greenish fruits, which resemble an avocado, mature in one season and generally drop in October and will germinate soon thereafter. Fruits from trees on high slopes are frequently washed down by autumn rains, leading to dense growth of young bays along many narrow winding canyons. The thin-shelled "nuts" store well and are edible, but must be parched or roasted before using to remove the bitter taste. They may then be cracked and eaten or ground and molded into small cakes. I look forward to trying this when we have a bumper crop.

So look again at this common yet excellent broadleaf evergreen tree which has adapted over time to fire, flood and poor soil, reproducing successfully while providing food, flood-control and diversity in our hills and canyons.

TANBARK OAK—*Lithocarpus densiflora*

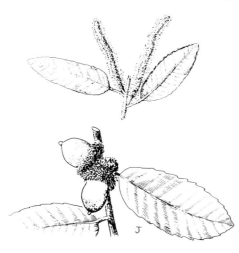

These are handsome evergreen trees easily overlooked because of their attention-getting neighbors, madrones and redwoods, but well worth getting acquainted with. Old growth trees are 150 feet tall with thick gray-green furrowed bark; young branches are quite downy. The medium-sized leaves are simple with straight veins from the mid-rib which end in small teeth on the edge. Full grown leaves are green, leathery and smooth on top. The underside is densely woolly, often with reddish-brown hairs. Leaves persist for three or four years. Tanbark's flowers, both male and female, are borne on new shoots of the year; the cylindrical male catkins are thick and erect and ill-smelling; the solitary female flowers are usually borne at the base of the uppermost male catkins. These and more details are why lithocarpus is not considered a "true oak." The fruit is a stout acorn maturing the second year after fertilization. The acorn is rather shallowly seated in a bristly cup. In fact one writer describes them aptly as looking as if "covered with brown Turkish toweling." Tanbark acorns were generally used for food by Native Californians, though perhaps a third choice after coast live oak and valley oak acorns.

This shade-tolerant tree is found in the coast ranges below 4500 feet on wooded slopes with redwoods, Douglas firs, madrones and bay laurels. Long an important source of tannin on the west coast, as chestnut was on the east coast, it was used in the leather industry. A man of my generation helped put himself through college up north by stripping tanbark every summer.

George B. Sudworth who did his excellent field work about the turn of the century says, "Tanoaks are thought to be a connecting link between oaks and chestnuts." They grow with redwoods, madrones and bay laurels, trees which Elna Bakker and other community-oriented ecologists call "the mixed evergreen forest...(which) came into being during the confrontation of the two great Tertiary floras, Arcto- (northern) and Madro- (southern) and has elements of both."

Now that there are many, many more of us than when our shoes were made mostly of leather, it is a relief to know that other sources of tannin have been developed. Hooray for the "good fortune" of the tanbark trees, may they grow large (150 feet tall) and old (those we see are mostly second growth trees up to 85 feet tall). Who knows if we or our children may have to look to their acorns for food again as Native Californians formerly did?

SANTA LUCIA FIR or BRISTLECONE FIR— *Abies bracteata*

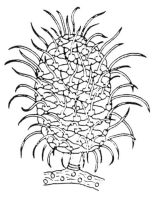

Our original criteria for choosing which plants to include in this regional book were those commonly found and showy or beautiful. This tree is beautiful but not at all common, but we include it anyway. See photo (page C-9) in our color section. It is one of two planted trees, probably 40 or 50 years old, growing in the Forest Service's Cerro Alto Campground one mile off Highway 41 between Atascadero and Morro Bay. I greatly admire these trees and have called attention to them on the numerous hikes I've led in this rich wild area for many years.

Like its other fir relatives, Santa Lucia fir's female cones stand erect on high branches, the bracts and cone scales fall with the ripe seeds, and the needles (leaves) have no stalk. Unlike other firs, Santa Lucia firs are tall and narrow, tapering abruptly into a steeple-like top; the lower branches hang almost to the ground; the two and one-half to four inch long cones are remarkable for the bracts which give the cone a very bristly appearance; the needles are spine tipped, mostly two-ranked and dark green.

Santa Lucia fir is an outstanding example of an endemic plant, i.e. limited to a particular geographic area. This handsome tree is found only in the Santa Lucia Mountains of Monterey and San Luis Obispo Counties. They occur in an area approximately 45 miles long and about one mile wide. About 11 or 12 populations are known from the headwaters of Carmel River in the north to near Cambria in the south.

These attractive trees are very isolated from any other species of fir. Their nearest fir relatives are found approximately 225 miles to the north, about 50 miles to the east and more-or-less 120 miles to the southeast. In their range they mingle with redwoods, madrones, California bays and oaks, seldom making a pure stand. A good place to see them in the wild is along the Cone Peak trail off the Nacimiento road.

When I first explored the Santa Lucia Mountains, I observed these lovely rare endemic trees, and gathered much of the above information from Helen K. Sharsmith. She was a botanist then at the herbarium at U.C. Berkeley who was also on this week-long horse-pack trip in April of 1971. It was a memorable experience in so many ways, one I'd love to repeat with six or seven kindred spirits. If you, dear reader, would be interested in joining such an expedition, send me a postcard in care of the publisher.

WESTERN HUCKLEBERRY—*Vaccinium ovatum*

I found this small, stout, evergreen shrub on the north-facing slope of Hazard Peak in Montaña de Oro State Park. Looking up from the canyon, they reminded me of the rounded forms of sheep grazing above us. When we arrived among them, there were a few pinkish-white bell-shaped flowers peeping out from under the shiny, leathery tooth-edged leaves and I knew we'd found an old friend in the Heather Family. They probably are "pruned" here by the prevalent salty winds. North in the Santa Lucias, they grow taller and erect under tan oaks and madrones along the sheltered, sun-dappled trails in the forest. There they make more flowers in small clusters, which hang shyly under the rather horizontal leaves. Western huckleberry occurs in the outer coast ranges from Santa Barbara County north and blooms any time from January to June. If you happen along on the right day in early fall, you may get to taste a tart-sweet blue-black berry or two! They remind me of the wild blueberries I gathered in Michigan in cut-over woods and from canoes along the swampy edges of inland lakes. Of course these huckleberries don't hold a candle for taste to those tiny, but numerous blueberries of childhood memory! The first domesticated huckleberries I saw looked obscenely large to me and they were not quite as delicious either, but they make pretty good blueberry muffins. When freeze-dry processing made them useful for backpacking in the high Sierra, how good they were hot over pudding, occasionally augmented with a few wild bilberries, a mountain cousin to our vaccinium.

Marjorie C. Schmidt recommends western huckleberry for shade gardens. They like acid humus soil and a little morning sun. We hope to try a few small bushes under the lovely big pine tree behind the Morro Bay Library. They won't look like grazing sheep here, but they'll have acid soil and hopefully endure the strong afternoon winds.

CALIFORNIA HONEYSUCKLE—*Lonicera hispidula*

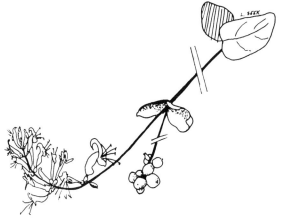

Frequent in cool shaded canyons or on moist hillside ground, this sprawling vine which lacks tendrils clambers over other bushes along the coast in all three counties of our area. California honeysuckle's green leaves are rounded and the upper pairs are fused together encircling the stem. The pretty pink whorls of flowers grow on the ends of the vine's branches and the rather lip-shaped petals roll back somewhat when the conspicuous stamens are mature. These are followed by dull red rather succulent berries.

There is another very attractive honeysuckle, *L. interrupta*, with spikes of yellow flowers, which is more woody and less vining that grows on dryer chaparral-covered hills. It seems to overlap with *L. hispidula* especially in Monterey County. Last winter I found a dozen or more long vine-like branches sweeping the ground from high in the trees along a truck trail in Julia P. Burns Park. Many had tiny roots at the nodes. Swaying back and forth in the sea breeze, there didn't look to be much chance for vegetative reproduction here. So I snipped a sprig with two nodes, brought it home and planted it in the shade in my yard. One stands there with the same few leaves, the other node grew and now has climbed up a five foot wire fence. It's hard to wait to see if "my" honeysuckle will have yellow or pink flowers—¿quien sabe?

BUTTERCUP—*Ranunculus californicus*

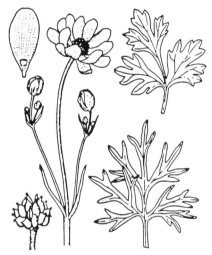

There are many butter-cups, but we chose to include here this common and very attractive one, a perennial herb with bright green lobed and divided leaves and shining yellow flowers on up to two foot stems. The sepals are the same color as the petals and together they may look like ten or more petals, but there is a nectar gland at the base of the petals only. Buttercups have many stamens and pistils in the center. In the ovary at the base of each pistil there develops after pollination a one-seeded fruit which was relished by Native Americans.

Ranun-culus means little frog and many members of this genus grow in wet places where frogs may also be found. This buttercup and its relatives may be found in many communities and after moist winters may be seen blooming from February on into May.

Buttercups call to my mind shining yellow "faces" scattered among meadow grasses or gleaming in clusters in sunny openings in the woods of our coastal mountains. But come slip back with me to the memory of a nippy spring morning at Rancho Santa Ana Botanic Garden where I was ambling along the path by the stream with part of a fifth grade class. One young man spied a nice group of buttercups blooming under the buttonwillow bushes, so we paused and enjoyed his discovery. As we moved onward, he said to me, "You must have sprayed those buttercups with plastic before we got here, didn't you?" I can't recall now any specific reply beyond, "No, they are naturally shiny, etc." (The "shine" is due to light reflecting from starch grains in cells near the surface.) Now I muse over how lucky some city children are to make personal discoveries in nearby botanic gardens and how lucky we are to live up here, where shiny buttercups are a common part of our springtime walks.

STARFLOWER—*Trientalis latifolia*

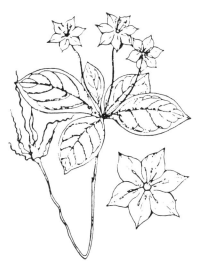

This slender little member of the Primrose Family grows in shady woods, often close to the sea, from San Luis Obispo County north. Rising from an underground tuber, there is a whorl of four to six regular green leaves up to eight inches above the ground. From the center of the leaves a loose cluster of one to four pinkish white star-like flowers rise, each on its own slender stem. The sepals, petals and stamens make a regular design pattern. Starflowers were more numerous than I've ever seen them under chaparral along the Cerro Alto trail in May of 1991 after the copious March rains.

Marjorie C. Schmidt lists Pacific starflower as a ground cover in well-watered shady areas.

Trientalis = 1/3 of a foot for the height; latifolia = broad-leaved.

ELK CLOVER or CALIFORNIA SPIKENARD— *Aralia californica*

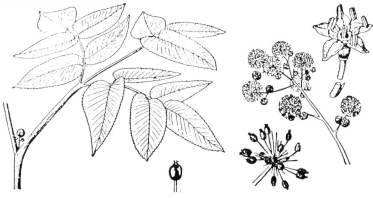

Spikenard is probably only a look-alike for other members of the Ginseng Family which are important in Asian cultures. Nonetheless it is an interesting and very attractive large plant along streams and around hillside springs in all three of our central coast counties where it blooms from May on into July.

Elk clover commonly grows three feet high or more from a large root which contains a milky juice. It has large compound leaves which turn a golden yellow some years before falling. The many-flowered umbels stand erect and each tiny white flower on its own pedicel becomes part of this symmetrical globe. I find this plant most attractive in autumn when the purple-black fruits stand on their red stalks in sharp contrast against the huge sprays of foliage.

An eastern relative of our aralia has a strongly aromatic root, which has been used as a substitute for true sarsaparilla, forming the basis for some of the flavoring in root beer. True sarsaparilla—*Smilax officinalis*—grows in Honduras. Northeastern Native Americans formerly used this false sarsaparilla root as an emergency food only, as it's rather strong if eaten directly.

FALSE or BRANCHED SOLOMON'S SEAL— *Smilacina* spp.

This lovely member of the Lily Family is commonly found in moist shady woods in all three of our central coast counties, often near the coast.

False Solomon's seal has a terminal cluster of numerous small white flowers, sometimes fragrant toward evening (nocturnal pollinator perhaps?). The blossoms top a long stem which also produces two rows of parallel-veined, tapering leaves. These lilies are perennial herbs with thick creeping underground root stocks.

Both the reddish-purple or spotted red berries and the starchy aromatic roots are edible. Do read on before starting to salivate: cooking the bitter-sweet berries removes most of the purgative they contain; the roots (dig only on private property with permission) must be soaked overnight in lye to remove the bitter acids and then the lye must be removed. Now you can cook them!

You may find various species of false Solomon's seal. One in all our area is *S. stellata* var. *sessilifolia*, pictured here, which has lance-shaped leaves and fewer flowers. Munz says that some form of false Solomon's seal may be found from the Pacific Coast to the Atlantic shore, so many of you will be meeting an old friend when you find "ours" in the woods from February to May.

ALUM ROOT or CORAL BELLS—*Heuchera micrantha*

Heuchera (pronounced héw-kera) is an entirely American genus of the Saxifrage Family. Sixteen are native to California. Several grow in our area and north. We chose *H. micrantha* because we've found it often in this community where it grows on shaded rocky banks of the coast ranges.

The common name, alum root, refers to its long woody rootstocks which have astringent and medicinal values. (I remember as a youngster being given, by my pharmacist uncle, a piece of alum to lay inside my lip where I had a canker sore. It cooled it down and dried it up!)

This compact plant is very attractive with evergreen palmately-veined and lobed leaves, which are often a bit hairy with the veins showing reddish color. The quite tall, slender stems support a feathery panicle of small white or pinkish urn-shaped flowers.

Alum root has come cheerfully out of the woods and into our gardens where it is frequently called coral bells. "White coral bells upon a slender stalk..." I can still hear the Brownie Scouts singing that familiar round. Marjorie C. Schmidt describes five cultivars. My favorite is Santa Ana Cardinal: clumps of rounded green leaves with scalloped edges; flowers small, urn-shaped, freely borne on tall wand-like stems and rose-red. They bloom May to July, but were ever blooming at Rancho Santa Ana Botanic Garden.

Hybrids are vigorous, strong growers, requiring only moderate amounts of moisture in sheltered, shady locations. Their geographic backgrounds in the wild are truly amazing. For example: Santa Ana Cardinal is a cross between *H. maxima* from the Channel Islands and *H. sanguinea*, from which the garden coral bells was derived, is native to Arizona, New Mexico and down into old Mexico! I find it refreshing to realize that some of our nature tampering is at least aesthetically good.

FAIRY BELLS—*Disporum* spp.

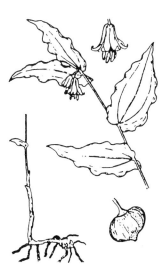

Nodding or peeking out from under their large, wavy-edged, parallel-veined leaves, fairy bells are a fine discovery in shady moist woods in February. I've never found them very far away from redwood trees. One to five greenish-white flowers occur on branched stems which grow to over two feet long. We say long rather than tall, because they tend to ramble sideways over and around the other often lush vegetation. These perennial members of the Lily Family grow from slender rootstocks and make red fruits, usually about May. Be sure to watch for this attractive, but not too conspicuous, moist woodland plant.

STREAM ORCHID—*Epipactis gigantea*

This woodland lovely may be discovered in cool wet places by creeks, marshes and seeps at the low elevations of western parts of our three counties in March and on to July some years. The flowers are rather large, as wild orchids go in California, up to an inch or more in diameter. They have concave sepals and purple or reddish petals; the lip is veined and marked with purple-red. Under the sepals you'll find the twisted ovary characteristic of the Orchid Family, rising on its short pedicel out of an upper leaf axil on tall stems. The visibly parallel-veined leaves are large near the base and smaller up around the flowers. Stream orchid has a creeping rootstock with fibrous roots.

I first saw this attractive flower in bloom at the botanic garden in Claremont. It was quite a time before I was able to spy them out in nature. When walking trails in the habitats described above, watch for the tall leafy stalks somewhat reminiscent of corn lily foliage, then carefully look closer. The flowers are not tiny, just well camouflaged!

PHANTOM ORCHID—*Eburophyton austinae*

"...Charming orchids which may appear as ghostly phantoms in wooded areas. The plants are perennial saprophytes arising without green leaves from a creeping rootstock. They are entirely white and may stand from 16 to 20 inches high with white leaves wrapped around the stem. The Latin word ebur means ivory, and phyton, a plant. This is a genus with one species. It may be found in May or June along the trail to Redwood Spring near the summit of the Nacimiento road to the coast."

—Beatrice F. Howitt, *Wildflowers of the Monterey Area*

I have yet to find this orchid in our area, but hope to.

EVERGREEN or REDWOOD VIOLET—*Viola sempervirens*

    Everyone loves violets, tame or wild, and there is a special reward for those of us who leave Highway 1 and walk into the cool shady woods where these wildings seem to fit so comfortably. The half inch long lemon-yellow flowers grow, one to a stem, two to four inches tall, above the evergreen, almost hairless, heart-shaped leaves. Both leaves and flowers arise from short under-ground scaly rootstalks which also produce stolons (stems) which run through the damp forest litter to start new plants. Blooming from January to August, I have found them flowering in February very near the sea, where the redwoods follow canyons down to tiny coves along the Big Sur coast in Monterey County.

10. VERNAL POOLS

INTRODUCTION TO THE COMMUNITY

Vernal pools are shallow basins that fill with winter rainwater which is either slowly absorbed or evaporates or both. Over eons of time, various plants and animals of this mini-community have adapted to this rather brief time when their basic necessities of life are available, i.e. moisture, sunlight, soil and warming temperatures. The seeds of many vernal pool plants germinate in the fall and wait out the winter as partially dormant rosettes. These tiny plants grow very little while covered with water, but when it recedes they grow quickly, flower and set seed in spring and early summer.

Vernal pools occur in several coast range valleys in our three county area, though most lie in grasslands on the east side of the great central valley of California. Others are found on level areas in chaparral, oak woodlands and even coniferous forests. As these pools dry, various wildflowers grow and bloom in concentric circles around the shrinking water. Elna Bakker in *An Island Called California* describes typical circles of goldfields, Johnny tucks, meadowfoam and popcorn flowers with downingia in the lowest zone. Other writers have likened these circles to bathtub rings.

My first encounter with downingia was quite different from what I expected. At the end of an all day field trip, we moved cautiously by flashlight along the muddy edge of a road between Jolon and Highway 101. The flowers were blooming thickly on the hummocks between deep water-filled cattle footprints, which reflected our lights up on the blue downingias. The scene reminded me of the hummock-water mazes one sees at the upper silting-in end of many small high Sierran lakes. Also playing vital roles in these brief mini-worlds are amphibians, fairy shrimp, salamanders, spadefoot toads, migrating shore birds and water fowl. We mention here one classic tale of co-evolution, between a specific goldfield plant and its pollinator, a solitary bee in the genus andrena. When the goldfields bloom, the female andrena gathers balls of pollen to deposit in her underground nest. On each ball she lays one egg. The larva hatches and eats the pollen. It pupates and emerges as an adult only when conditions are right again.

Several vernal pools have been protected by the Nature Conservancy and other groups concerned about maintaining natural systems. More need to be, like the thoughtful rancher who fenced off a corner of his pasture, which included a pool, so his cattle would not trample it, as had the cattle in my first encounter. Their unique conditions seem reason enough, but here is yet another reason: vernal pools may some day provide society at large with important products. The seeds of meadowfoam, for example, have recently been found to contain an oil nearly identical to sperm whale oil, which is highly prized as an industrial lubricant because it retains its viscosity at high temperatures. For more excellent information and fine colored pictures, see Sarah Steinberg Gustafson's fascinating feature article "Ephemeral Edens" in the spring 1990 *Pacific Discovery*, a journal of the California Academy of Sciences, San Francisco.

Several relatives of vernal pool plants are treated elsewhere in this book. Here we have drawings of four plants which have been found in our three counties in the recent past. Some documented locations are very likely "peopled over" now, so it behooves us to find other locations and get them set aside.

Downingia cuspidata

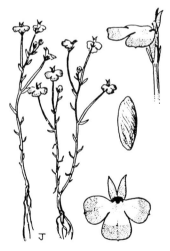

This most frequently found vernal pool flower has no common name, but is a member of a genus in the well known Lobelia Family. Note in the drawing the long inferior ovaries that reach from the sepals down into the axils of the stem leaves. The flower has a two-lipped blue and white corolla, the lower lip being much enlarged. There is a front view rendering in color on the California Native Plant Society Spring Wildflower poster and in the "Ephemeral Edens" article, mentioned above.

MEADOWFOAM—*Limnanthes douglasii*

Helen Sharsmith (see "Further Reading List") provides the following derivations: Limnanthes, marsh and flower, for habitat and habit; douglasii for David Douglas, famous Scottish plant explorer, in California from 1830-1832.

Other flowers in this category are *Boisduvalia densiflora* and *Eryngium armatum*.

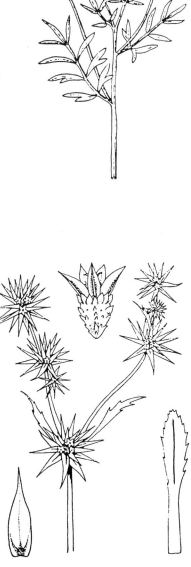

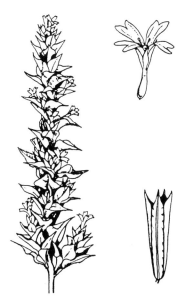

Boisduvalia densiflora

Eryngium armatum

11. FIRE FOLLOWERS

The very pleasant aromas that come to our noses as we push off-trail through scrub and chaparral are volatile oils which are also very flammable. In fact these communities plus oak grassland, foothill woodland and redwood forests, which typify much of the geography of our three counties back from the sea, are very fire prone areas. The tinder dryness of accumulated dead debris during much of the year, coupled with natural lightning-caused fire and the practices of Native Californians who lived here for thousands of years before us, helps us realize that the vegetation here has evolved with and made many fascinating adaptations to fire. Since prehistoric times, the Ahwahneechee of the Yosemite Valley burned the grass understory vegetation at the right time most every year, to facilitate their harvest of the all-important acorn crop under the oak trees and also to open visibility so they'd be less likely to be surprised by unseen dangers like bears which also ate acorns. Then we came along with our protectionist concept for managing our national treasures and prevented all fires for many years in the valley. The tremendous buildup of fuel and an accidental fire produced an intense, slow moving holocaust that killed oaks and much other life. It is clear we need to relearn about fire what the old ones had known for centuries.

Many plant ecologists think of fire as taking the place of fungi as recyclers of dead wood and other normal plant discards in a dry climate such as ours. The ash left on the ground after fire contains basic nutrients which enter the soil and are very quickly available to the roots of plants making new growth. This was fascinating to observe along the northwest end of the west Cuesta Ridge of the Santa Lucia Mountains after the Highway 41 fire of August 1994. California Native Plant Society leaders conducted hikes for the public there twice a month from October 1994 to February 1995. The autumn rains were gentle and frequent. Crown sprouting, new seedlings and plants forced into premature bloom, such as yuccas, currants and tassel bush were found along the Cerro Alto trails. Ken McCall, writing in the county newspaper after his second February hike, put it thus: "And all around us the land was slowly coming back." Wildflowers in April, May and June were profuse and lovely.

In early 1995, heavy rains caused gullying, erosion, flooding and costly damage to property. We need to understand that we cannot totally control natural forces like fire, floods and earthquakes, but we can learn to adapt to them. Large acreage developers, county boards of supervisors and individual homeowners in places like Tassajara Canyon, please note! We ask too much of our valiant fire-fighting crews, out of short-sighted ignorance.

Some plants such as redwoods need bare mineral soil on which to germinate their seeds. Others need periodic fires to heat the seeds enough to scarify the seed-coat—matilija poppies, bishop and knobcone pines and sargent cypress are in this group. True, the fires open the cones of these "closed-cone-pines" so the long-mature seeds can scatter; they also heat-treat the seeds, enhancing germination.

Dr. Hoover writes in his *Vascular Plants of San Luis Obispo County* of the "remarkable fire-type herbs, annuals and a few perennials which appear in profusion the year after a stand of chaparral is destroyed by fire, but otherwise germinate sparingly if at all." The dynamics of fire has interested me since I found many knobcone pine seeds scattered thickly among the ashes on the slopes of the San Bernardino Mountains above Redlands on one of our Botanic Garden training course field trips just days after a fire.

We've already discussed some plants' adaptations to fire in previous pages, see: bush poppy (p. 51), Indian warrior (p. 58), madrone (p. 123), star lily (p.24), fiesta flower (p. 120) and yerba santa (p. 29). Other examples follow below and on the next page.

FIRE POPPY—*Papaver californicum*

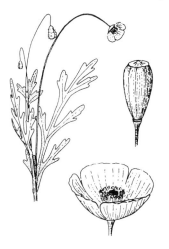

These dainty orange-red, four-petalled flowers with green centers, nodding buds and slender finely-haired stems are very numerous after fire only. Their tiny seeds may survive as long as 50 years before germinating and reproducing after the next fire. They are related to oriental and Iceland poppies. Though smaller, they have nodding buds, hairy stems and seed pod anatomy in common.

Fire poppies should not be confused with our state flower, California poppy—*Eschscholzia californica*, or with the collarless poppy—*Eschscholzia caespitosa*, the colorful blanket on east Cuesta Ridge which many folks thought had been planted. They had not, but their seeds remained from a previous fire.

TWINING SNAPDRAGON—
Antirrhinum kelloggii

This is an attractive pinkish-lavender to violet flower which is common after fire. A typical Figwort, this dainty annual has five petals which form a tubular throat, belling out into two lips. Not typical are twining snapdragon's very slender flower stems which rise out of its leaf axils and tangle up with every nearby plant in the resprouting chaparral, even with tall grass stems.

SLENDER SUNFLOWER—
Helianthus gracilentus

This large handsome sunflower was conspicuous all along the west Cuesta Ridge the spring and summer after the Highway 41 fire, occasional to absent before. A perennial from a thick root, slender sunflower has opposite leaves with stiff hairs on both surfaces. The disk flowers vary in color from yellow to reddish-purple, while the ray flowers are consistently yellow. The large garden sunflowers are relatives of this native genus *Helianthus*.

WHISPERING BELLS—
Emmenanthe penduliflora

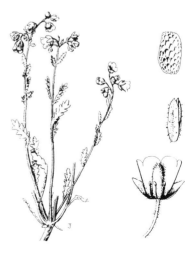

The flowers are recurved in numerous rounded clusters, and are light yellow-green. The dead flowers do not drop off, but, dry as paper, they rustle in the breeze, hence the common name. These much-branched, sticky, scented annuals with mainly narrow pinnate leaves are in the Waterleaf Family, kin to the showy baby blue eyes and fiesta flower.

EPILOGUE

I see many hopeful signs that we are becoming aware of our dependence on this fragile planet for our own survival and that the rights of other living organisms must be recognized as equal to our own. Stewardship and enlightened exploitation must be the watch words of the 21st century which is right around the corner.

Happy trails.

—*Mary Coffeen*

FURTHER READING LIST

Abrams, Leroy. *Illustrated Flora of the Pacific States: Washington, Oregon and California* (four volumes). Volume IV authors are Abrams and Roxana S. Ferris. Stanford: Stanford University Press. Volume I, 1940, 538 pages. Volume II, 1944, 635 pages. Volume III, 1951, 866 pages. Volume IV, 1960, 732 pages. This extensive four-volume flora is profusely illustrated with black and white drawings. It has value for non-botanists because the contents page of each volume gives the family names in English as well as Latin, so we can leaf through a family looking at the pictures. Also, Volume IV has an index of common names for all four volumes.

Bakker, Elna S. *An Island Called California.* Berkeley/Los Angeles/London: University of California Press, second edition 1984, 455 pages. If you read this book from cover to cover when you first get interested in wildflowers, you'll experience a whole new approach to the natural world. I trust it will enrich your wanderings as it has mine, and enhance your understanding of the natural systems that support all life.

Balls, E.K. *Early Uses of California Plants.* Berkeley/Los Angeles/London: University of California Press, 1962, 103 pages. An oldie but goodie and useful, I've heard, to Native Americans searching for their cultural roots, as well as to us interested gringos.

Barbour, M.C., R.B. Craig, F.R. Drysdale and M.T. Chiselin. *Coastal Ecology: Bodega Head.* Berkeley/Los Angeles/London: University of California Press, 1973, 338 pages. Excellent hows and whys for the plants and animals that live along our shores, as well as at Bodega Head.

Barbour, M.C., B. Pavlik, F. Drysdale and S. Lindstrom. *California's Changing Landscapes.* Sacramento: The California Native Plant Society, 1993, 256 pages. The book discusses the diversity of our vegetation, its conservation and restoration where it has been damaged.

Clarke, Charlotte Bringle. *Edible and Useful Plants of California.* Berkeley/Los Angeles/London: University of California Press, 1977, 280 pages. This interesting book is a useful addition to Balls' *Early Uses of California Plants.* There are recipes for filaree frittata and no-bake health fudge! The author, a knowledgeable botanist and gourmet cook, is also a backpacker who probably tried everything she wrote about.

Connor, Judith and Charles Baxter. *Kelp Forests.* Excellent publication of Monterey Bay Aquarium Foundation, 1989, 64 pages. Beautifully illustrated with color photos and written with both knowledge and a sense of wonder about representatives of the intricate webs of life in this aquatic world.

Dawson, E.Y. and M.S. Foster. *Seashore Plants of California.* Berkeley/Los Angeles/London: University of California Press, 1966, 1982, 217 pages. A good reference to take along on beach and bluff walks.

Hickman, James C., Editor. *The Jepson Manual: Higher Plants of California.* Berkeley and Los Angeles: University of California Press, 1993, 1400 pages. The ultimate resource for scientific names.

Hoover, Robert F. *The Vascular Plants of San Luis Obispo County.* Berkeley/Los Angeles/London: University of California Press, 1970, 350 pages. A technical flora, but less difficult to use. Valuable for location checks of the flower at which you are looking. A color supplement was published by the San Luis Obispo Chapter of the California Native Plant Society. It was produced by friends of Dr. Hoover after his untimely death. 1974, 160 pages.

Howitt, B.F. and J.T. Howell. *The Vascular Plants of Monterey County.* Wasman J. Biol. 22: 1-184. For California Academy, 1964, 184 pages. A technical flora, valuable for geographic occurrence.

LeBoeuf, B.J. and S. Kaza. *The Natural History of Año Nuevo.* Pacific Grove: Boxwood Press, 1981, 425 pages. This very interesting book has good information on plants which are also found in our areas further south. Thirty of the fine drawings in Chapter 3: Land Plants were done by a young friend of mine who died recently of cancer.

Lenz, L.W. and J. Dourley. *California Native Trees and Shrubs.* Claremont: Rancho Santa Ana Botanic Garden, 1981, 232 pages. This is a valuable book for both information and for its many beautiful color photographs. The emphasis is on native plants for ornamental horticulture, but it also deals with environmental considerations such as our water problems, which are not going to go away, even if it rains! The book is based on over 50 years of data and experience.

Meeuse, B.J.D. *The Story of Pollination.* New York: The Ronald Press Company, 1961, 243 pages.

Meeuse with Sean Morris. *The Sex Life of Flowers.* New York: Facts On File Publications, 1984, 152 pages. Both of these books are great for plant and pollinator relationships. The recent one is based on a PBS

Nature presentation. The first book is perhaps less "sexy" but well illustrated and fascinating.

Munz, P.A. and D.D. Keck. *A California Flora.* Berkeley/Los Angeles/ London: University of California Press, 1959, 1681 pages. This technical botany book was produced for Rancho Santa Ana Botanic Garden. It has valuable drawings on the first page of each family. This book was the official flora for California for 34 years.

Munz, P.A. *Shore Wildflowers of California, Oregon and Washington.* Berkeley and Los Angeles, 1964, 122 pages. A good beginning book. Due to its reach, we don't find all of our area's wildflowers in it. Excellent black and white drawings showing a distinctive characteristic, e.g. a seed pod, or close-up of one flower, or a leaf cross-section.

Niehaus, Theodore, F. *A Field Guide to Pacific States Wildflowers.* Boston: Houghton, Mifflin Co., 1976, 432 pages. A currently popular field book. Like many botanists, he has resorted to using part of the scientific name for the common name too often, but some of his common names I like because they are ecological, e.g. Seep Monkey Flower— *Mimulus gutatus.*

Raven, P.H. *Native Shrubs of Southern California.* Berkeley: University of California Press, 1966, 132 pages. Most of the shrubs of our area are found in this oldie but goodie. The "Check List" in the back in lieu of an index is of little use to the lay person, but you can always riffle through the pages!

Schmidt, Marjorie G. *Growing California Native Plants.* Berkeley/Los Angeles/London: University of California Press, 1980, 376 pages. A current, valuable guide for native plant gardeners.

Sharsmith, Helen. *Spring Wildflowers of the San Francisco Bay Area Region.* Berkeley and Los Angeles: University of California Press, 1965, 192 pages. The clear explanation of scientific names is very helpful to flower lovers.

Smith, C.F. *A Flora of the Santa Barbara Region.* Santa Barbara: Santa Barbara Museum of Natural History, 1976, 331 pages. A technical botany. Valuable for geographic occurrence.

Sudworth, George B. *Forest Trees of the Pacific Slope.* New York: Dover Publications, Inc., 1908, 1967, 455 pages. The soft-cover edition is an unabridged republication of the work originally published by the Forest Service of the U.S. Department of Agriculture. This classic treasure with its fine full page illustrations includes Fremontia, Dogwood and Christmas-berry or Toyon. It also includes a new table of changes in nomenclature.

GLOSSARY

Adventitious—Refers to buds arising from the surface of scarred or burned areas, such as damaged stems, branches, burls or roots.

Anther—In a flower, the sac and the pollen in it. Usually an oblong structure at the top of the filament.

Arborescent—Tree-like in size and/or appearance.

Axil—The angle between the stem and a leaf. Flowers often grow out of these axils; sometimes a tendril will also grow from the same angle. Example: Wild cucumber.

Calyx—The sepals of a flower as a group.

Composites—Plants with inflorescences which are actually composed of many ray (petal-like) flowers and many disk flowers in the center. (See Parts of a Flower diagram on page *VII.*) This Compositae/Asteraceae Family is one of the largest and most flourishing of all plant families. Example: Coreopsis, senecio, goldenrod.

Corolla—The petals of a flower as a group.

Cultivar—A variety or race that has originated and persisted under cultivation. The word is a contraction of culti-vated var-iety.

Cyme—A broad flat-topped or rounded flower cluster with the central flowers opening first. In cymes, the primary branches may branch again.

Decumbent—Lying on the ground with the tip ascending. Example: Beach primrose.

Dioecious—Having male element (staminate) and female (pistillate) flowers on separate plants. Examples: Coast tassel bush, pearly everlasting, willows.

Disjunct—In plants, a group or grove growing rather widely separate from others of its kind. Example: Western azalea.

Empirical—Relying or based solely on experiments or experience.

Endemic—A plant restricted in occurrence to a small section of a country or botanical province. Santa Lucia fir is an outstanding endemic in the California flora, which is noted for its high percentage of endemism.

Fecund—Fruitful or prolific.

Filament—The stalk of the anther.

Genus and Species Names—Most wildflowers have at least two names: a common name and a scientific name. The first one is what it is called right around where it is easily found. The same flower may be called something else over the mountain or a few counties north or south. The scientific name, however, is governed by the International Convention of Nomenclature and consists of a genus and species name which is accepted by trained botanists and the scientific community worldwide. If you want to learn more about a given wildflower, you must know the genus name to look it up in the published flora of its region. The species names used in this book are those found in the new Jepson *Manual of Higher Plants of California*. Since ours is a popular book for beginning flower lovers, we often use "spp.", which means more than one species.

Gland—A depression, protuberance or appendage on the surface of an organ which secretes a usually sticky fluid.

Inflorescence—A group or cluster of flowers on a single stem.

Monoecious—Separate male and female flowers borne on the same plant.

Nectary—A gland, secreting a usually sweet fluid, often appearing as a protuberance, spur or pit.

Ovary—The vessel for the developing seeds at the bottom of the pistil.

Ovule—The element in an ovary which develops into a seed.

Palmate—Having lobes or divisions radiating from a central point, like fingers from the palm of the hand. Example: Lupine leaves.

Penduncle—The stalk of a cluster of flowers. Usually flower-bearing pedicels arise from a peduncle.

Pedicel—The stalk of the individual flowers in a cluster or inflorescence.

Perfect—A flower having both stamens and pistil.

Petal—A usually bright-colored element located above the sepals at the base of a flower. Petals attract pollinators as well as flower lovers.

Petiole—The stalk which connects a leaf to the stem.

Pinnate—Like a feather. Having a main central axis with leaflets arranged in two lines on either side of it. Example: Rose leaves.

Pistil—The female element of a flower consisting of the ovary, one or more styles and the stigma(s).

Pollinium—In plants like milkweeds and most orchids, the grains of pollen from one anther form a compact, but not sticky, mass called a pollinium which has a sticky disk. These pollinia will attach themselves to a visiting insect which will carry them to the next flower.

Photosynthesis—The conversion of light energy to chemical energy; the production of carbohydrate from carbon dioxide in the presence of chlorophyll, using light energy.

Receptacle—The summit of a stem which bears a flower. In sunflowers, the enlarged summit of the stem bearing multiple flowers.

Recumbent—Leaning or reclining.

Saprophyte—A plant that does not manufacture its own food, but which needs decaying organic material as a source of nutrition.

Scarification—The scratching or breaking of the hard seed coat to hasten water absorption and germination.

Scorpioid—Rolled or coiled like the tail of a scorpion.

Seep—A place where water oozes from the ground to form a pool. Cienaga is Spanish for seep.

Sepal—The usually green element located below the petal at the base of a flower. The sepals encase the bud before the flower opens.

Spp—Used in this book for "many species."

Ssp—Sub-species.

Stamen—The male element of a flower consisting of a stalk (filament) and the pollen sac (anther) on top.

Stigma—The top of the pistil which receives the pollen.

Stolon—A horizontal stem running above ground, rooting at nodes and tip, giving rise to new plants. Example: Beach strawberry.

Style—The thin stalk between the stigma and the ovary. Often absent in wind-pollinated trees and shrubs.

Succulent—Any plant with soft and fleshy water-storing stems and leaves. Example: Live-forever/dudleya.

Symbiosis—Two dissimilar organisms in close association, particularly when that association is beneficial to either or both.

Umbel—Usually flat-topped clusters of flowers whose stalks arise from a common point, resembling the stays of an umbrella. Example: Poison hemlock.

Undulating—Having wavy-edged leaf or petal margins.

Viscid—Viscous or sticky. Example: Bush monkey flower.

INDEX

Index Key

- Common names are in Roman text, scientific names are in italics.
- The major reference to a plant is indicated by bold numbers, incidental reference by lighter numbers.
- Locations of color plates are in italics (e.g. *C-#, inside front cover,* etc.).
- Page numbers are listed only where that specific name appears (e.g. "sea rocket" is mentioned on pages 3 and 4, but its genus name "cakile" is only found on page 3).

DRAWING CREDITS

Linda Warren Seek: Giant Kelp (page 1); Beach Strawberry (6); Beach Morning Glory (7); Sand Plant (9); Giant Coreopsis (12); Sea Daisy (14); Mexican Sage (20); Toadflax (36); Mock Heather (37); Yucca (44); Pearly Everlasting (47); Pitcher Sage (54); Prickly Phlox (61); Matilija Poppy (62); Prickly Poppy (75); Prince's Plume (77); Baby Blue Eyes (81); Obispo Mariposa (84); Arroyo Willow (106); Brass Buttons (115); Poison Hemlock (115); Pacific Madrone (123); Western Huckleberry (128); California Honeysuckle (129); Phantom Orchid (135).

With permission from the Jepson Herbarium at University of California at Berkeley, from Jepson's *A Manual of The Flowering Plants of California*: California Poppy (13); Owl's Clover (23); Goldenrod (39); Chaparral Pea (46); Pink-Flowering Currant (56); Coast Tassel Bush (59); Valley Oak (69); Tidy Tips (79); Phacelia (80); Foothill Penstemon (96); Creek Dogwood (110); Twinberry (111); Snowberry (111); California Blackberry (112); California Bay Laurel (124).

With permission from the Regents of the University of California and the University of California Press, the following drawings were reprinted:

1. Philip A. Munz. *California Flora and Supplement*, ©1959: Buckeye (91); Western Sycamore (103); Crimson Columbine (116); Elk Clover (131).

2. Philip A. Munz. *California Spring Wildflowers*, ©1961: Blue Larkspur (11); Sea Thrift (17); Live-Forever (18); Star Lily (24); Chia (27); Suncups (28); Yerba Santa (29); Chocolate Lily (33); Wild Cucumber (33); Filaree (35); California Peony (41); Bush Poppy (51); Chaparral Currant (57); Indian Warrior (58); Woolly Blue Curls (59); Buckbrush (64); Tree Tobacco (71); Blazing Star (74); Popcorn Flower (78); Bird's Eye Gilia (81); Elegant Clarkia (82); Thistle Sage (83); Bladder Pod (87); Big-Leaf Maple (109); Western Azalea (113); Seep Monkey Flower (114); Milk Maids (117); Purple Nightshade (119) Fiesta Flower (120); False Solomon's Seal (132); Fire Poppy (141).

3. Philip A. Munz. *Shore Wildflowers of California, Oregon and Washington*, ©1964. Lupine (5); Bluff Gilia (16); Footsteps of Spring (18); Checker Bloom (19); Rein Orchid (20); Senecio (21); Black Sage (27); Wild Rose (30); Rose Mallow (31); Sticky Phacelia (39); Woolly Star (40); Buckwheat (42); Vetch (45); Mariposa Lily (83); Douglas Wallflower (94); Miner's Lettuce (95); Globe Gilia (97); Chinese Houses (99); Goldfields (100); Giant Trillium (119); Tanbark Oak (126); Stream Orchid (134); Evergreen Violet (136).

4. Edward Balls. *Early Uses of California Plants*, ©1962: Amole (26); Poison Oak (32); Hollyleaf Cherry (50); Manzanita (53); Toyon (55);

Jimson Weed (73).

5. Marjorie Schmidt. *Growing California Native Plants*, ©1980: Hummingbird Sage (28); California Fuchsia (34); Bush Monkey Flower (38); Indian Pink (41); Acorn Grinder (69); Douglas Coreopsis (77); Farewell-To-Spring (82); Scarlet Bugler (85); Wild Onion (86); Leopard Lily (118).

6. Helen Sharsmith. *Spring Wildflowers of the San Francisco Bay Region*, ©1965: Common Yarrow (10); Wild Iris (15); Blue-Eyed Grass (22); Wild Sweet Pea (46); Fiddleneck (76); Inland Blue Larkspur (92); Red Larkspur (92); Yellow Pansy (94); Red Ribbons (98); Shooting Stars (100); Indian Paintbrush (101); Fairy Lantern (117); Buttercup (130); Starflower (131); Alum Root (133); Fairy Bells (134); Meadowfoam (139).

7. Elna Bakker. *Island Called California*, ©1971: Redwood Environment Diagram (122).

8. Peter H. Raven. *Native Shrubs of Southern California*, ©1966: Deerweed (25); Fremontia (48); Coffeeberry (49); Climbing Penstemon (52); Clematis (60).

9. P. Victor Peterson. *Native Trees of Southern California*, ©1966: Mexican Elderberry (70); White Alder (108).

10. McMinn & Maino. *Pacific Coast Trees*, ©1963: Gray Pine (89); Black Cottonwood (104); Fremont Cottonwood (105); Santa Lucia Fir (127).

11. Dawson & Foster. *Seashore Plants of California*, ©1982: Sea Rocket (3); Sand Verbena (4); Beach Primrose (8).

12. Charlotte B. Clarke. *Edible and Useful Plants of California*, ©1977: Blue Dicks (16); Coast Live Oak (68); Milkweed (72).

The following drawings were reprinted from *Illustrated Flora of the Pacific States*, Volume III by Leroy Abrams, ©1951 and Volume IV by Abrams and Ferris, ©1960, with permission from Stanford University Press: Downingia (138); Boisduvalia (139); Eryngium (139); Twining Snapdragon (142); Slender Sunflower (142); Whispering Bells (142).